To Michael & Angela,

Hope this will be useful,

Love

John & Janie

Xmas 1974.

Golden Hands

Budget Brighteners for the Home

A ***Golden Hands*** *book*

Marshall Cavendish, London

Text David Fisher
Illustrations Kate Simunek
Editor Jeanne Sullivan

Picture credits
Steve Bicknell; Michael Boys; Camera Press;
Heidede Carstensen; Features International/
Godeaut/Francois Lamy/Perouse; Good
Housekeeping; Nelson Hargreaves; Graham
Henderson/Liz Whiting; Ken Kirkwood; La
Maison de Marie Claire; John Ledger; Chris
Lewis; Bill McLaughlin; James Mortimer;
John Sullivan; Jerry Tubby/Liz Whiting;
Ted Ward Hart;
ZEFA.
Cover picture: John Elliott
Designs by:
Susan Ayers; Crown Paints and Wallpapers;
Max Glendinning; Glynn-Smith Associates;
Julie Hodgess; Richard Morris.

We should like to thank the following for their
help in lending accessories for photography:
Armstrong Cork Company; Army and Navy
Stores; Berger Paints; Biba; Blue Hawk
Ltd.; (J. W.) Bollom; Bourne and
Hollingsworth; Business and Electronic
Machines; Casa Pupo; Chelsea Glassworks;
Christopher Wray's Lighting Emporium;
Coles; (J.) Crotty; Dan Klein; Davis
(Caroline) and Tordoff (Celia); Designers'
Guild; (The) Door Store; Dunlop; Furniglass;
Furniture Cave; Heals; John Lewis; Richard
Morris; Leslie Spitz; Liberty and Co.; Liden
Whitewood Ltd; Louvre Centre; Paperchase;
Pier 1 Imports; RTS Displays; Ryman Ltd;
Sanderson Wallpapers and Paints; Selfridges
Ltd; Strike One; T. F. Buckle; T. & S. Lemkow;
Tyne-Plaqs Co; Women's Home
Industries.

Front cover: Bedspread/Casa Pupo
Tumbletwist rug/John Lewis

Our thanks are also due to the following for
their kind co-operation:
Mr. Richard Rodney Bennett; Olive Sullivan;
Kenneth Tynan; Avery Wilson.

> Metric equivalents are given in brackets
> within the text. These equivalents are
> approximate only, and are intended as a
> guide to sizes and measurements.

Glossary of Basic Terms

Alkyd Paints: Water-based paints. These are
quick-drying and now are quite tough, but still
not as hard-wearing as polyurethanes.

Abrasive Paper: There are any number of
different grades and types of this paper —
i.e. flour paper, emery paper, garnet paper.
Ask your local dealer which type to use for
a specific task.

Enamel: Either a vitreous composition fired
over a surface to give a hard, gloss finish, or a
glossy paint which forms a hard, smooth coat.

French Polish: A traditional polish made
mainly of shellac dissolved in methylated
spirit.

Glaze: A very thin, transparent tint of colour
applied directly to wood or over a clear finish

lacquer. The term is used more generally to
mean any substance which will give a clear or
translucent shiny finish to a surface.

Japanning: To give a high gloss to a surface.
The term originates from the Japanese
technique of applying layers of lacquer
(usually black) to build up a shiny finish.

Polyurethane: Any of a specific group of
chemical compounds (polymers) used in
various resins, paints and lacquer finishes.
They give an extremely tough, hardwearing
finish.

Scumble: Generally speaking, a very thin coat
of opaque colour. In imitation wood graining,
a thin glaze which is applied in two layers —
a dark one and a light one which are combed
or blended together.

Spackle: A very fine filler for small holes or
dents in wood surfaces. Available in a
proprietary mix. Decorators often make their
own from finely ground plaster of Paris,
linseed oil and a tint.

Thixotropic: A technical term used by many
paint manufacturers to indicate that a paint
is non-drip.

Varnish: A term used to denote a clear
protective finish. There are many different
types — some based on wood resins, others on
synthetic cellulose constituents and others on
shellac and a volatile spirit mixture. Modern
'varnishes are usually made of clear plastic
lacquers.

Wood Stain: Either a chemical mix or a
proprietary mix which alters the colour of
wood. There are natural tints and brilliant
colours.

Published by Marshall Cavendish Publications Limited
58 Old Compton Street
London W1V 5PA.

© Marshall Cavendish Limited 1973
58 Old Compton Street
London W1V 5PA.

This material was first published by
Marshall Cavendish Limited in:
50 Colourful Ideas for Painting and Decorating
Second-hand Furniture Made New

This volume was first published 1974

Printed by: Petty & Sons Ltd., Leeds
Bound by: Acfords, Chichester

ISBN 0 85685 046 2

This volume is not to be sold in the USA, Canada
or the Philippines.

Contents

About this book...

Is your home as bright and attractive as it could be? Don't you sometimes feel that it is well overdue for a facelift, but don't know how or where to start.

This Golden Hands book is packed full of ideas for reviving faded room schemes and bringing second-hand furniture to life – all illustrated in glowing colour to give you plenty of inspiration.

See what unusual effects can be created with paint, wallpaper, fabric, tiles or wood stains by using these materials in an imaginative way. Then discover the secrets of renovating old furniture to complement a new room setting, from re-finishing a scratched table to re-upholstering chairs and sofas.

Curio collectors will find invaluable information on cleaning and mending china, glass, silver, pewter, chrome, copper and brass. Everything, in fact, to turn those bargains into handsome additions to your home.

To ensure that you get truly professional results from your decorating and renovating, the easy-to-follow instructions are accompanied by step-by-step diagrams.

Giving your home a new look doesn't have to cost the earth. You will be amazed how easily and effectively the dullest decors can be transformed into cheerful rooms full of bright furniture and well-cared for treasures. So save money and live colourfully.

1 Cover: Clever use of decorating materials can make a simple room setting look impressive. In this room two completely different patterns are combined — one in fabric; the other in paper. The colours are bright and cheerful, creating a mood that is modern, fresh and practical: a bedroom to be lived in.

2 Below: Careful colour scheming is sometimes the best way to give a room unique appeal. Here the walls have been painted in a cool yet striking green, offset by narrow bands of blue and by the cream ceilings and woodwork. These colours, echoed by the mural and accented by red and yellow, make a co-ordinated look.

1

PAINTING FOR SHINE

Paints with a shine to them have a long history, and a reputation for being the most effective protection against the atmosphere that can be put on with a brush. Since they were for a long time more expensive than other paints, as well as being more difficult to apply, they have come to be regarded as the natural finishes for woodwork—and similar, small, hard-wearing areas in the house.

It still makes fairly good sense to employ gloss paints for their utility value, but they do have intrinsic virtues other than sheer toughness. They come in every colour you could wish for, for one thing. And for another, their shine gives enhanced depth and brilliance to the shade you choose.

Gloss colour values
Wherever you put a dark-coloured glossy paint, you give the surface you coat a mirror-like quality. Although there are many situations in which mirror-like reflections would detract from the overall effect, there are others where they can add interest and sparkle.

Remember too that by thoughtful grouping of colours you can achieve pretty well any degree of harmony or discord in a room's general atmosphere. Monochromatic harmony is arrived at by more than one tone of a single colour. To imply supreme calm the different tones should be arranged in order of intensity, so that your eye travels naturally from light shades to dark, or vice versa. For example, if you decide to paint a series of panels or stripes you could start with yellow and go on through yellow-green, green, green-blue, blue, blue-purple in that precise order, without introducing a single jarring note. But change any pair of them, one with the other, and you will have discord.

Working chosen dominant colours with judiciously placed contrasts usually makes for more life in a room, but even in this kind of scheme you can control the degree of contrast by moving slightly away from directly contrasting colours and using accents instead. Some helpful colour scheme ideas appear on page 64.

Alkyds
Of the four main groups of glossy paints in common use, the alkyd-resin based finishes are still the bread-and-butter line. No matter whether calling itself a lacquer, an enamel, a fine-finish or a simple hard-gloss paint, if your can is not carrying a label stating that the paint inside is based on some other substance, it will almost certainly fall into this group. Alkyds are easy to apply, will stick happily to most other finishes, can be had in just about any colour under the sun, and are made in enormous quantities. They are, therefore, likely to be reasonably priced wherever you buy them.

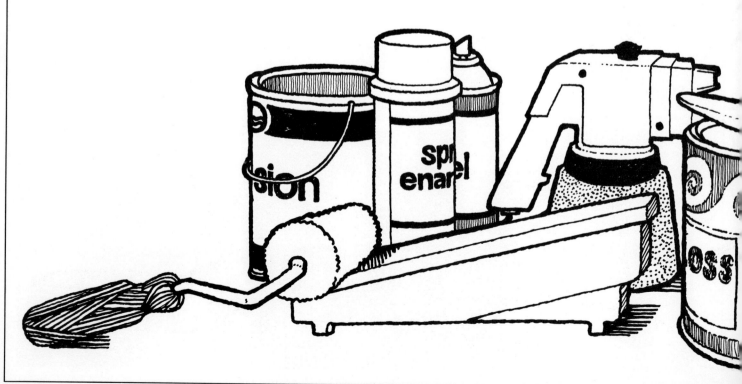

Variations in the factory mix can give alkyd paints special characteristics for special jobs. Some have surface-sealing properties for priming unpainted work, and others have exceptional opacity which makes them ideal undercoats for the glossy paint used for finishing (which can be more translucent than the thicker one-coat paints that are meant to do triple duty).

Polyurethanes
Made from a far tougher resin, the newer polyurethane paints are at the same time harder, smoother and more flexible than alkyds, but they only give their best performance when there is *no* non-polyurethane paint between them and the surface.

Emulsion gloss
Emulsion gloss forms a group on its own, being the only water-borne gloss finish in existence. Although a plastic emulsion paint, its gloss is comparable to that of an alkyd. For painting heating radiators it is unsurpassed, drying quickly and giving off no odour once dry—even when the radiators get hot.

Many quick-drying paints are based on alkyds, but if the drying-time claimed by a manufacturer is under one hour, you can be pretty sure that it needs professional skill. It may be based on nitrocellulose, as car-body re-touching lacquers are, and so be easy to put on, but poisonous.

Washing
Manufacturers usually specify ideal preparations which they insist must be carried out if their paint is to give satisfactory service, but you can take much of what they say with a biggish pinch of salt. Paints in all four main groups can adhere firmly to any surface free from loose dirt, grease, oil and wax. This means sponging over with a cleaner made and sold specifically for pre-painting work, used at the dilution recommended for painting preparation. Most can be used at half-strength for merely cleaning down, but you want a proportion which will etch the surface for you a little.

Rinsing off the cleaner is absolutely necessary, but you do not need to create an indoor monsoon to do it. Half a gallon of clean, cold water in a bucket will be enough for a surprisingly big area. Wipe a small section at a time with your sponge rather wet, squeeze it almost dry under the water, and wipe over the same place again. Change the water when it begins to put dirt back.

Rubbing down
Once you have washed down like this, and allowed the surface to dry, your paint will stick. Further work is optional, unless there are gaping holes to fill or a great deal of embedded grit. On an average surface, a light rubbing with medium-grade (100 grit) glasspaper will suffice. After this you should have a fairly continuous base to work on, patchy to the eye but smooth to the touch. If it still shows major blemishes such as small cracks or peeling of previous finishes, stripping down to the raw material will be easier than trying to abrade down to sound paint. If you think you may need to use a primer or undercoat, check the paint can for the manufacturer's recommendations.

Stripping
Whereas stripping is only rarely necessary, it is far easier than you may imagine. Chemical paint removers soften old coatings so that they can be scraped off without much difficulty. In the process, however, they contaminate whatever was painted so that you then have to wash it down as well.

Burning-off is not the fire hazard that it was in the days of petrol blow-lamps. Put notions of professional-style tricks firmly behind you—make no attempt to follow your modern gas torch flame closely for long stretches with your scraper, and you will be safe. Keep the flame moving, backwards and forwards over short stints—under 12in. (305mm)—so that the whole warmed surface lifts. Then turn the flame away into safe airspace and keep it there while you scrape. Paint melts off easily, but use chemicals for old varnish.

USING TWO COLOURS

Having chosen the shine you want to put on and prepared the surface to take it, you have to decide which of the methods of applying the paint is right for you. Brushing is still by far the most popular and usually the most practical method. For every awkward corner or seemingly inaccessible strip, there has been developed a set of bristles in a convenient holder which will help you to reach it. Get a helpful brush and you are at least halfway to success.

Brush action

Brushes hold paint between their close-packed bristles by means of surface-tension, which is broken whenever the bristles move against each other allowing paint to flow towards the tips.

All paint should leave the brush via the tip, never from the sides. The basic action, used for 90 per cent of the time, consists of trailing the brush tip along behind the handle, then tilting the whole brush over so that you can trail it back in the reverse direction.

Pressure should be light but firm, and the brush should be lifted briefly clear of the surface at the end of each pass, with the tilting taking place in the air.

Cutting-in

The opposite technique, for cutting-in paint on inside angles or on moulding corners, may be thought of as using your brush as you would a spade when breaking fresh ground. However, instead of following the action through, you convert the stroke back to a trailing one as soon as paint has been firmly poked where you want it to go.

Runs at panel corners occur when cutting-in strokes overlap and the brush is overloaded. Halfway up the length of the bristles is the farthest you

should dip, ever—even with thixotropic paint which will be discussed more later. Always use the cutting-in action to draw excess paint away from inside angles and panel corners. To avoid blob-collections where outside angles are formed by intersecting planes—be they straight, curved or fluted—trail the brush towards the cliff edge and follow through completely off it so that unwanted paint leaves with the bristles, instead of being squeezed off to dry in blobs. Repeat for the other surface forming the angle.

Border techniques

Outside angles are the most convenient places to organize borderlines between one colour and another. The brush technique is exactly the same, but you must clean it very thoroughly, in a modern solution preferably.
Other essential success factors are:

1 Letting one colour dry hard before you apply the next.

2 Putting on the lighter colour before the darker.

3 If using more than one coat of each colour, finish one sequence before starting another, except for priming paint, which you put on everything before you undercoat anything.

Should you decide to pick out (say) the panels of a door in a different colour to that on the rest of it, the problem is a little more difficult. One way out would be to let the parts surrounding the panels dry fairly hard so that you can safely use a low-tack masking tape (a special product, not standard masking tape). If your hand is at all unsure of itself, use this method, because as a rule, you will have to contend with a deepish, narrow groove between panel moulding and door-frame member.

Different surface borders

Where your gloss line borders on masonry, as it may around the architrave of a porch door, you will most likely have to follow freehand the outer edge of a strip of mortar, or mastic sealant. Paint your own line slightly short of that where the mortar meets the masonry. Yours may not be absolutely straight, but it will certainly be straighter than the one you 'follow'. The only mistakes noticeable will be blobs and jerks, so take your time.

Always outline the edge of an area before filling in the body of it. Work in short, easy stints, forgetting the return-trail stroke and always pulling the paint along in the same direction. Stretch a string or soft wire across your paint pot so that you can wipe all excess colour from the three sides of the brush tip not in contact with the surface.

Never stand on tiptoe, or reach. Paint from a secure, balanced stance. Holding your breath on the ticklish bits helps a lot. If you are right-handed, work from left to right on long,

horizontal lines (vice versa if you are left-handed). Where you can, paint upwards on vertical lines. If you are in an agitated frame of mind, put off painting borderlines until you feel calmer.

By far the easiest inside-angle paint line presents itself when you are painting to meet wallpaper. Here you can tuck paint right into the angle, even splosh harmlessly on to the wall to a small extent; not too far, though, or you may spoil your chances of good edge-adhesion when you hang the wall-covering.

Wall paint/gloss borders

When you have to make wall paint and gloss meet neatly, put the gloss on last, and do a smooth, freehand edge just short of the angle. This is relatively easy because you have an outside angle to guide your bristles. Newspaper, clean and uncreased, is ideal for keeping paint off the floor when you reach the bottom of the skirtings. If you take a flimsy one, fold it double to make a stiffer edge.

Near glass, you need masking tape and care combined, especially for frosted glass. With leaded lights or panes careful freehand painting is the only reliable method, but you can paint clear, flat glass with abandon, following up by scraping it clean after the paint has dried.

3 Opposite left: Use two colours to give added dimension to a room. The plain white doors in this instance have been given extra depth, by painting the panels yellow and outlining them in a slightly darker colour.

4 Opposite right: An alternative idea for using two colours is just to hint at the second colour, by painting in fine outlines on doors or panels. Here, the pictures make an interesting frame for the door area.

1. Take care when painting door stiles not to scrape any blobs off the brush on to the top edge. Place the bristle tips very precisely when you start a stroke at an edge or corner; something you should not do with a full brush. Work some of the paint on to the body of what you are painting before finishing its extremities. 2. Since you will already have painted the surrounding mouldings, you need to spread paint into the panel edges which abut them. Be economical to avoid unevenness and runs.

3, 4. A window brush, with bristles cut at a convenient angle, is extremely useful for mitred mouldings and other tricky corner work. It has considerable advantages over a broad brush for narrow-fluted mouldings. Although slower, the results it produces are likely to be well worth the extra time. On some edges it can be helpful to use the window brush upside down. In this position it makes the painting of skirting-board bottom edges (where they meet the floor) quite a bit less awkward than it is with a straight brush.

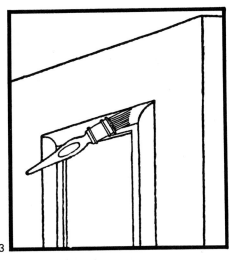

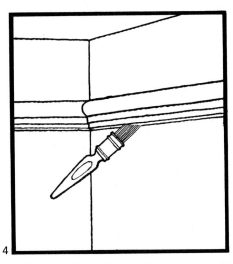

MATT-FINISHED SUBTLETY

Just as glossy paints have beauty and virtues all their own, so do matt ones. Light striking a shiny surface is reflected off mostly in one direction, but light falling on a matt surface is refracted in all directions. Oddly, this characteristic makes matt surfaces somewhat brighter than glossy ones of the same colour, because the light leaving them travels less far, staying nearby and doing a very useful job in the process.

Lighting points
Being less obtrusively reflective than gloss paints, matt ones are inevitably more generally acceptable for broad expanses of wall or ceiling, where they make the most of whatever light falls on them. Darker colours absorb a great deal of the light available, some as much as 98 per cent of it. Consequently, though you may want them for their atmosphere of richness or mystery, you must accept that they will considerably darken a room in daylight, and that the level of artificial light you will need to provide after dark may well be increased by several hundred per cent.

In this context, bear in mind the basic home truth that every theatrical producer learns early in his career: that no matter how much light he has on a stage he must never spread it evenly all over, or the set will appear unbelievably dingy. He may concentrate the light on the backdrop, to throw figures into sharp relief; or he may put pools of light where the action is taking place, on an otherwise dark scene. Either way, his intention is to provide a focus of interest, to create meaningful contrasts, putting your attention where he wants it.

Remember that tungsten light is a good deal yellower than daylight, and fluorescent light bluer, so experiment a bit with colours you mean to use lots of. Look at dried dabs of them under the lamps in the room in which they are to go before you commit yourself to painting.

Daylight, of course, changes colour at different times of day and produces different effects on colours according to the way a room faces. Rooms with windows facing cold light (north and east in the Northern hemisphere, for instance) can be brought to life with warm, rich colours, while those with a warm or sunset aspect can exploit their more generous ration of warm light with cool or neutral shades.

Using colours
Look at your room as a blank canvas and decide first of all what sort of atmosphere you would like it to have, then organize its looks to produce that atmosphere. Human sensitivity to colour is great, and different shades are able to excite impressions of sound, fragrance and states of emotion as readily as they may induce spatial freedom or claustrophobia.

It is not possible to offer rules which would determine the effects specific colours will create, because people differ widely in their response to any given shade. Start by considering the colours you feel happiest with and believe will work well in combination. Try to find examples of room decorations which have used the colours you want, to check the over-all effect produced. If you find it hard to visualize the finished results, play safe with a neutral background and add accenting colours in furnishings and accessories until you get the atmosphere you want. Or use different tones of the same colour, employing the darker shades to bring some surfaces nearer, and lighter ones to push looming ones reassuringly back. This technique can alter the apparent shape of any room providing that the contrast between light and dark shades is sufficiently marked.

Types of matt finish paint
Between dead-matt and high-gloss paints, there is an enormous range of finishes. Until plastic emulsion appeared, the cheaper concoctions of animal-glue, water, and white lime or powdered colours were the only economic alternatives to flat oil paints, except for the harder-wearing and less dusty oil-bound distempers. These and flat oil finishes make good bases for modern paints, requiring only thorough cleaning (see page 4). In much older houses, you may have to paint on top of the more crumbly whitewashes or distempers. After washing these down seal them with a binding primer before putting on the finish you want.

Emulsions
Flat oil paints are still on the market, and still the mattest you can get. However, since they do not resist dirt or condensation as well as more modern matts, you may prefer a tougher plastic emulsion which has a slight sheen. Straight emulsions also offer a fair degree of porosity, allowing the surface beneath them to dry out but not to get wet again—hence their widespread use on new plaster walls. These, though, should not be painted when very wet, and certainly not until any salt formation (efflorescence) has stopped. Thin the first coat down with water as much as the manufacturer recommends.

Vinyl emulsions
Similar in character, but with a silk-like texture, are the newer vinyl emulsions. These are even tougher, and some have an acrylic content for brilliance and permanence of colour.

Alkyds and polyurethanes
Both alkyd and polyurethane paints come in eggshell-surface formulations, having very pronounced sheens. The alkyd ones usually take longer to dry, but the polyurethanes, like their glossy cousins, do not reach maximum hardness for about a week. By the time they have cured, they are the toughest of the tough, and very good-looking into the bargain.

Blackboard paint
In children's rooms, or a general living area, you may want to use part of a wall, or plywood/block-board panel as a blackboard. For this job, you can get special paints, but straight plastic emulsions are totally suitable in any of the very dark shades of green, brown, blue or even black.

5 Above: The flat, non-reflective quality of matt-finish paints is often best employed in rooms where a subtle blend of colours is the desired effect. In this room the brown of the carpet is continued up the lower portion of the walls, and the yellows and reds of the furniture are repeated in the upper wall areas. Such a division of colours is particularly effective in rooms with high ceilings.

6 Right: In this study the plain timber boarding has been painted in a soft, matt-finish blue, thus enhancing the appearance of the unusual window screen.

TEXTURING

There are many ways to create surface interest on walls. Colour is only one of them; texture is another, often more unusual.

7 Below: A marbled effect can be obtained by mixing oil-based paints and applying them over a base of linseed oil, as described in the text. The best results are achieved by working on flat panels and then fixing these to wall areas.

8 Right: Special plastering techniques, simple even for amateurs to do, can be used to disguise faults in a bad wall. When properly applied such a surface makes a suitable, plain background for wall decorations.

Large scale motifs and coarser textures are probably more effective than the more restrained treatments when you create your own patterns in cellulose filler. Bold designs are also likely to prove easier to carry out, small irregularities not being noticeable. If you want to make your own implements, plastic laminate is a good material. It can easily be sawn or filed into interesting edge shapes, and it is extremely hardwearing. Avoid tools with thick edges for this kind of work because they will pick up too much filler, clog up too often, and may spoil the pattern.

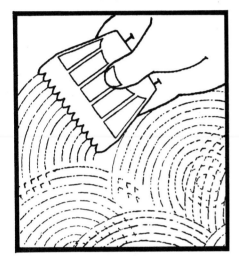

A textured surface is distinctive and different, but its very permanence brings with it the corresponding need for exceptionally careful consideration of sites and designs. Broadly speaking, you should avoid deeply indented, bold textures in confined spaces and small rooms. To decide whether or not a space is confined, stand back somewhat from the surface you want to treat. If it can be viewed from a distance which allows you to see the length of an imaginary line drawn diagonally across it, you can safely carve it to your heart's content. But if surrounding walls or other obstructions force you closer, it may be advisable to scale your ideas down a little.

Disguising faults
Texturing can be resorted to for other than aesthetic reasons, of course. It may be a useful way of disguising a wall flank or a ceiling that is cracked or uneven, or edges which are inexpertly patched and undulating, showing ridges where old plaster meets new. You may decide to resort to texturing as a very much easier method of resurfacing than conventional, 'fair-face' plastering. With so much surface interruption on view, irretrievable irregularities must be really gross before they stand out as unintentional.

Materials to use
Materials to help you impose your kind of texture on a surface are readily obtainable (within the bounds of civilization, at any rate) and normally no more difficult to manage than alternative kinds of decoration.

Finer degrees of texturing can most easily be achieved by paints which themselves have a texture, unlike the ones normally used for inside surfaces. Cement-based paints, such as Snowcem, can be pressed into service, but with certain provisos: they do not like other paints underneath them, nor plaster, nor distemper, nor even limewash. And they can attack hard gloss paint while they are still wet, so spillages need instant wiping. Some resin-based texture paints can be put on top of cement-based paint, but read all the tins and leaflets, just to make sure.

Paints containing sand or stone granules are not so fussy about the materials they will stick to. In fact, they are probably the most tolerant of all as regards surface preparation. Most will happily accept emulsions over them once they have dried, but this should rarely prove needful as the choice of colours is a bit wider than that for cement coatings.

As a rule, stone/sand paints have great elasticity, which enables them to seal and fill hair cracks as you brush them on. Like all totally non-porous finishes they need a fungus-free surface. Although many of them contain fungicides, you just may be unlucky enough to find an interior wall or ceiling with mould on it, in which event you may need to use a separate fungicide beforehand.

Exterior mixes
Various exterior rough-cast/tyrolean mixtures can be used in the house to good effect. Usually they come in the form of ready-formulated powder/granule mixes, to which you add water to make a slurry. This may be put on by trowel or by hired, portable machine. More than likely, these products will be cement-based, in which case cautions already indicated apply.

Plaster and filler finishes
Alternative materials, perhaps cheaper but nonetheless effective, are patching plaster (browning, not finishing) and ordinary cellulose filler (e.g. Polyfilla). These are mixed with water into a stiffish mortar, and applied with a trowel on to your chosen surface as evenly as possible. Neither stays workable for longer than an hour, so work in limited areas, using half the time available to you for trowelling and half for imposing your will on the newly laid mix.

Stippling with stiff brushes, rolling with patterned rollers, combing with coarse combs or with nails knocked through pieces of wood, indenting with jar or bottle necks, or with food cans can all be carried out quickly and easily. Fingers or old cutlery, shaped sticks of wood or a dozen other implements can help ring the changes, leaving you with absolute originality of surface to paint as you like when it is dry. If you would rather have an interesting finish straight from the trowel, mix small gravel with your mortar so that the dragging and rolling of the pieces, as you spread the mixture on a wall or ceiling, scores random trenches.

Marbleizing
The very special effect created by this paint finish is not a very difficult one to produce, but does require patience and care. It looks best in small areas and is easiest to apply to flat surfaces, so think in terms of single wood panels to be fixed to the wall later. Do practise your technique before committing yourself to the real thing; a piece of marble or a good colour photograph will prove an invaluable guide.

Prepare the surface by rubbing down well; use a woodblock wrapped first with a medium grade glasspaper, and then with a fine grade. Select two or three colours in an oil-based paint—one for the background, the others for the marbled effect. Gloss finishes work better than matt ones. Apply the background colour and when this is thoroughly dry, wipe lightly over the surface with a soft pad of cloth dipped in linseed oil.

Now use a small dense sponge to apply the second colour, spreading the paint lightly over the areas you want to cover. Always use a gentle pressure and concentrate on a circular swirling motion. The third colour should be applied straight away, preferably with a feather, as a brush gives too precise an outline. Drift this colour into thin lines or gentle blobs, allowing the oil to blur the colours together if you like. You can now use another dry feather to blend the colours into further patterns; your reference guide will be most useful here. Further drops of paint or of a mineral turpentine substitute may be added—the turps will create a 'negative' effect through to the base coat. Allow to dry and wipe away any excess linseed oil that has not been absorbed.

COLOUR IT STRIPED

Try thinking of stripes in a new context. Stripes were fairground tents, stripes were awnings, were candy, pyjamas and flags of all nations; too razzmatazz, too bold and too flashy for the solid, comfortable background of the place where you live. Stripes can be colour, life and warmth, or cool tranquillity. Always, they attract and lead the eye along, so naturally act more happily as emphases than as background patterns.

Using stripes

Why not consider stripes, or panels of paint on paint, as an imaginative, original means of breaking up the commonplace, boring, bald expanses of single colour walls and ceilings which have become traditional in boxy modern dwellings? Equally, why not use them to bring to life to a lofty, perhaps dreary, turn-of-the-century house, whose only claim to 'period' status is its age? One surely need have little fear of spoiling such a building with out-of-date decor.

Living-places are there for the benefit of people, not people for buildings. The lords and barons knew this when they built their castles, the landowners when they built their manors, and the merchants when they put up magnificent town-houses. Many of these dwellings were extremely beautiful, but all were created by imaginative people doing the best they could with the materials available to them at the time. Unfortunately for their imitators, much of their philosophy died with them.

Many of these imitators of manorial splendour have given us such false images of good taste as dark varnish and porridge wallpaper. Oak panelling was too often translated into brown paint, and hand-carved cornices into factory-made plaster mouldings by such persons.

Good taste lies in harmony, contrast, colour, shape and texture, all managed into proportion and unity with each other. If you inherit a true and unspoiled period dwelling, you may well feel that you have an artistic duty to restrict wilder impulses so as not to damage its essential character, and rightly so. But if your dwelling is less than a 'period piece', all's fair in your fight to make it habitable and suit your personal needs.

Fashions in decor

Mankind seems to have a natural desire to fill in blank spaces. Cave murals and carved panelling are historical examples of it and decorating fashion cycles result largely from this urge. When things start becoming too cluttered, or circumstances dictate particular needs, people tend to wipe the blackboard clean and reinstate clean lines and uncluttered surfaces, so allowing the cycle to repeat itself. Such a utility phase took place in many areas following the Second World War, and trends in most areas are now well on the way back to doing something about naked spaces.

Panels and stripes enable you not only to add interest to spaces, but to change their apparent shape completely. Vertical stripes can make a wide space look narrower, while horizontal ones may have a widening, lengthening effect. Stripes can emphasize a door, a window, an arch or an alcove. Panels can provide similar emphasis, or they can break up the separate entities of wall and ceiling by continuing from one to the other.

Using masking tape

Working on sound surfaces, properly prepared, you can use modern masking tape to control areas of almost any shape of colour-strand or patch. Large arcs of freehand-looking colour zones are possible, and you do not need an artist's fist to achieve them. If you do venture into random patterns and sizes, though, you do need an innate sense of balance and proportion.

Your surfaces need to be base-coated with really good-quality, high-sheen paint before you start masking, since even some of the special low-tack pressure-sensitive masking tapes (NOT ordinary masking tape) may pull standard emulsion away. Think, then, in terms of a vinyl emulsion or an eggshell finish, and do not start until it is hard dry. It is inadvisable to try masking on an area that has a lining wallpaper on it—it is very apt to pull away. Be sure to test the tape on a small, unnoticeable patch, before you begin.

Techniques for working

Mark out for vertical lines with a plumb and chalked string, and for horizontals with a good spirit-level. Stick your tape to the lines in short stages, about a foot at a time. As it does not easily go around corners, curves are best done by sticking broad tape over the entire bend-area, marking the curves with a string-and-pencil-type compass, and then cutting the tape carefully with a craft knife. Peel off the strips that are to be painted. Make sure none of the tape edges remain unstuck, or paint will seep under. Press them down with fingers or a small paperhanger's roller.

The longer you leave the tape stuck, the harder it sets, so paint as soon as you have fixed the tape down. Use a thixotropic type of paint (gel-like) so that you will need to paint only once, and remove the tape as soon as the paint is touch-dry. This technique not only makes your tape easier to peel, but leaves your stripe or other feature with a raised edge, which throws it into sharp relief.

9 **Opposite: Decorating schemes need not be restricted by the rigorous use of colour in large, flat areas. Use shape as well as colour and you will find that ideas for redecorating a room abound. Painted stripes are only one of many possible alternatives. Make them thin and elegant to provide relief around a door or window. Or, as this picture shows, splash out and make them bold and exciting for a child's playroom.**

1. The string on the plumb has been well rubbed with chalk— coloured if the wall is too pale to show white marks clearly. Let the

1

2

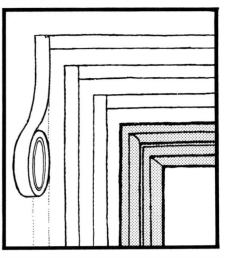

3

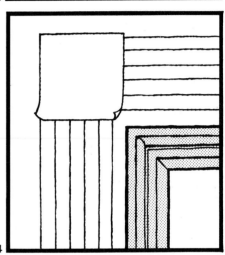

4

5

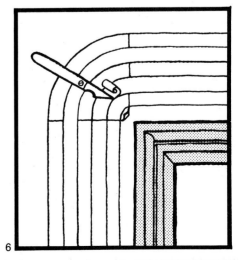

6

weight come to rest naturally, then trap the string near it against the wall; gently so that it does not move sideways. Pluck it firmly away from the wall, being careful not to deflect it right or left, and let it go.
2. A longish spirit level is the easiest answer to the problem of getting horizontal lines. The level's long sides are parallel to each other, so provided the bubble is centred between the appropriate marks on the vial in the middle, lines drawn against either side will be correct. When picking up starting marks on the wall, allow for the thickness of the pencil point. 3. Stick the tape on a little at a time. You can still feed it straight from the roll, so that your fingers do not need to touch the adhesive side too much. Cut it gently with a very sharp knife.
4. Special broad tape is needed for the corners if you want to radiate the stripes around them. Lay a generous piece over the whole bending area so you leave no gaps.
5. String and pencil make an efficient pair of compasses. Adjust radius by shortening string. 6. Cut freehand around radii with low-angle or convex blade.

CUT-OUT SHAPES WITH STENCILS

In an age which offers so much that is ready-made, more or less on-the-wall-straight-from-the-package, stencilling may at first seem outdated—a waste of time and effort. Like striping and panelling, however, decorative stencils are worth doing precisely because they are not done by someone else, indeed cannot be reproduced exactly by anyone except you.

Equipment
A stencil is by definition a thin mask, with predetermined shapes cut out of it which allow the passage of colour or other marking through to the surface against which it is held. Bearing in mind the necessity of making stencils yourself, you need to work with material that is thin enough to cut by hand, stiff enough to be used without framework, flexible to some extent, so that it will conform to surface undulations under light hand pressure, and sufficiently impervious to the paint you use to remain serviceable for the number of times you want to use it.

Making your own stencils
Strong cartridge paper, such as good quality posters might be printed on, will serve well enough for very limited usage, but your choice of sources probably means that what you use will already have been printed on. A test will tell you whether or not the ink is likely to bleed through. Cardboard from cereal packets is another possibility, although the same precaution is needed with that.

Tissue paper
Relatively thin sheets of tissue paper can be made to work extremely well. The trick is to glue them together using a PVA, white woodworking adhesive (such as Evostik Resin W) diluted roughly 1 part water to 3 parts glue. When the glued tissues are dry, they are incredibly strong. Setting time is only two hours or so.

Wallpaper cut-outs
Vinyl wallpaper makes good stencil-fodder, provided it is not ready-pasted, of course. With this you may have the distraction of a busy pattern, difficult

to ignore while cutting out totally unrelated contours, but it is possible to make this ready and willing design work for you instead of against you. Wallpaper is especially good to use as a pattern for growing-foliage themes, otherwise very difficult to arrive at. Just cut out the parts you want—and throw them away ! The resultant painted shape will not breathe a hint of wallpaper.

Plastic clear sheet

Any firm of commercial stationers should be able to supply you with thin, clear plastic sheet, which is used to protect wall charts and maps. This is perhaps the ideal material for heavy-duty stencils, but always test with the paint you use to make sure its solvent has no adverse effect.

Cutting and templates

To ensure clean outlines and corners when cutting out stencils, use a sharp craft-knife with a low-angle or convex blade. You may find you can get better shapes by drawing around templates first, then cutting freehand—always against a firm underlay which will not mind knife cuts : possibly thick layers of newspaper, or scrap hardboard. If you are a fair hand at freehand drawing, you will need neither templates nor pointers as to what you can use for outlines, but there are many common household objects which can be used.

While you could scarcely expect to produce impressive abstract forms without innate artistic ability of some sort, there is no reason at all to discount the possibility of fabricating more than reasonable flowers, leaves, trees and similar outlines using such things as eggcups, wineglasses, coasters, walking-sticks, hairbrushes, mincing-machine cutters, shoe-trees, coat-hangers, scissors and pastry-cutters as sketch-templates.

Since your base coat will be painted already, drawing pins should not be used for holding the stencil while you paint, so use the low-tack masking tape recommended for stripes to fix the edges. You can then hold each cut shape in close contact with your base with one hand and paint with the other. Where there are large cutouts to fill in, you can line in their edges with a fine brush, take the stencil off the base and fill in the shapes free from strain.

Aerosols

Aerosol spray paints can help you to achieve both speed and uniformity with stencils. But remember that the stencil needs to have ample borders for spray painting, to accommodate scattered paint.

10 **Try one of these stencil graphs, following the instructions on page 14. The picture opposite illustrates the dramatic effect.**

FUN WITH MURALS

In a great majority of minds the word 'mural' may conjure up a picture of a large fresco, painted long ago by a master hand, its once brilliant hues now fading decadently beneath the dust. Mural is in fact a very loose word, meaning any kind of wall decoration, although with distinct pictorial overtones.

Size and pictorial quality are what distinguish a mural from mere panel decoration. A mural is the height of presumption in interior decor—either dominating its surroundings as it should or ridiculing itself, which it will do if its setting gets the better of it. To spell out the message in full: plan your mural first, then the surroundings to suit it.

Murals have traditionally been hand-painted, and if you are a dab-hand pictorialist you will have no trouble in producing in-situ original artistry. The Michaelangelo in most of us is missing, however, so those who set their hearts on imposing wall pictures may be forgiven for turning to twentieth-century technology and considering photographic ones.

Photographic murals
That is not to say you need wave good-bye to hopes of originality, or even of uniqueness, as it is very possible for an experienced amateur with a camera in the Rolleflex, Leica or Pentax class to attain negatives or transparencies good enough to be professionally enlarged to at least six feet by four. Some of the larger photographic dealers and processing houses offer this facility as a standard service, and most of them do big enlargements for industrial publicity purposes, so have the know-how.

Such an enlargement would come to you mounted on stiff board, which would itself need to be mounted on even stiffer board. Impact adhesives are useful for mounting these large panels, which cannot be screwed or nailed. Ask the processers which ones to use because many contact glues contain solvents which damage photographic emulsions. They are also the best people to give you advice about clean-ing, varnishing, polishing and other maintenance.

Mounted brass rubbings
Photographs are by no means the only self-help wall pictures needing no personal artistic skill. Carefully done series of brass rubbings can look very striking, cut out and mounted on a sizeable white background. Many churches will not allow you to take aluminium foil impressions of memorial brasses, but if you can obtain such moulds, with honour and diligence, you can make dramatic figures for mural decoration by pouring cream-consistency plaster-of-paris into them, having first turned up the outer edges. When it has set, mount the thin plaques on to hardboard sheets—they are easily stuck with cellulose filler mixed to a smooth paste. Such reliefs can be sprayed with metallic or other colours.

Outline techniques
Artists of doubtful proficiency can use household aids to achieve steady curves and profiles similar to those suggested for making stencils, but larger. Tennis or squash racquets, hockey sticks, vacuum cleaner hoses, flexible plastic curtain rail, all make good curve templates for chalking in outlines.

Making a graph
In some situations, nursery walls for one, you may want to reproduce some figures from a small, printed original. Try tracing it on to squared graph paper, then copying the sketch, square by square on to enlarged squares drawn in the scale you want the finished picture to be. Suppose the original tracing is on $\frac{3}{4}$ in. (19mm) squared paper, covering a space 3 in. (76mm) wide by 4 in. (102mm) high, and you want to enlarge it to about 3 ft. (1m) by 4 ft. (1.2m). Start by chalking out an oblong this size on the wall, mark yourself a 3 in. square grid within the area and proceed to copy out the design, one square at a time. If you use chalk to make the picture, you can easily wipe off any mistakes before you paint. Vinyl emulsion paints are best to use, especially if you use masking tape.

As an alternative to painting on the wall, try painting on thin pieces of wood or hardboard and mounting these on to the wall.

Marquetry pictures
Should you have a genius for jigsaw puzzles, and a steady craftsman's hand, you may well be attracted to marquetry and learn to make wood-veneer murals, piece by painstaking piece. Of course, you must have a feeling for wood and a practical bent, but a good book will give you the basic knowledge, and if you confine yourself to simple shapes, avoiding the intricate detail that is beyond your skill, patience will make you pictures.

Lighting points
A little thought and trouble taken with lighting a mural pays constant dividends in the enjoyment of it. Spot lamps are unlikely to do such a flat feature justice, nor are fluorescents, unless you can get hold of a true day-light-colour tube. Tungsten strip lighting should offer the best chance of combining drama with detail visibility, but the tubes would need to be put behind simple shields to avoid glare.

Right: Vibrant colours are usually at their best in a plain and spacious setting such as this one. The wall mural has been planned on and cut from thin hardboard, while the table-top displays a repeating pattern to unusually good effect.

Projectors may be aimed square-on to get accurate representation, or askew for special effect. Some of the picture will be badly out of focus if you overdo the tilt. Remember that few projectors have cooling systems good enough to allow slides to be screened for more than a minute or two and survive undamaged. You will need to angle your marker to trace projected outlines because of the shadow problem.

If pipes and other similar house functions must be left open to view, decorate them so that the eye is deliberately drawn to them, instead of merely noticing them as unsightly obstructions.

12 Right: A fireplace grating can be made to blend in perfectly with surrounding walls, and may then be used as a centre of focal interest.

13 Below: Imaginative and unconventional colour-scheming has been used here to distract the eye from the awkward shapes and bulges of the pipes.

PAINTING EXPOSED FUNCTIONS

The great variety in shape and size found in examples of exposed functional equipment in homes (e.g. pipes, heating equipment) makes it possible to isolate only two likely problems—they may well project into your living space, and they will almost certainly be hard to get rid of.

Perhaps you may have no legal right to plot their destruction because they belong to your landlord. On the other hand, they may be yours for life but less trouble to put up with than to remove. It may be very dangerous to interfere with them, or they may be too useful to move. Just occasionally, you come across one so intrinsically attractive that your only concern in painting it is to make the most of its good looks.

Paint, with its proverbial ability to cover up a multitude of sins, is likely to prove the most effective means of disguising, integrating or improving the monstrosities or miscellaneous, potato-faced fittings which intrude their presence into your life. The first step to dealing with one is to decide whether it is basically a beauty or a beast, remembering always that the beast in the fable became a handsome prince as soon as he got the right treatment. Having made up your mind to pick it out from its background, or to merge it by using an identical or similar colour, choose your finish and work backwards from that.

Preparing the surface
Establish what it is made of. If the material is wood, copper, brass or bronze, you may have the option of scraping or cleaning down to a respectable layer so that new good looks can be sealed away from further degradation. Clear polyurethane lacquers are a natural choice for this job. Remember to de-grease thoroughly between cleaning and sealing. Your problem may, of course, have been painted already, and it may be possible to re-paint without stripping the old coats, if they are firm and reasonably sound-surfaced. Some older metal fittings may have acquired over the years an attractive patina which only time can produce, so careful cleaning without abrasion can pay handsome dividends in their case. Clear sealing usually adds nothing but enhancement.

Wood
Wood functions are few, but you will come across some ceiling fixtures and switch mounts in early nineteenth-century property, the majority of them deserving little more trouble than a coat of paint. As a rule, they fit in with their background well enough if they are painted to match the room's woodwork rather than to blend (hopefully) in with paint or wallpaper. Sparing coats, applied with patience and a small, soft brush will give you a clean outline against paint on wall or ceiling. If you are papering, of course, you will paint these small items at the same time as the rest of the woodwork, beforehand.

Exposed roof trusses and rafters in attics may well be worth some perseverance to rescue them from unmerited oblivion. Diligent scraping may well bring to light the seashore grain of seasoned Douglas fir. Should their surface prove too scarred for reclamation, work down to a firm base and paint with emulsion, perhaps dramatically darker than the rest of the ceiling.

Copper and lead pipes
Large-diameter pipes are best made a feature of with wallpaper (see pages 56-57) but small ones succumb satisfactorily to paint. Copper and lead do not take at all easily to being painted. Primers are a waste of time, so thorough pre-paint cleaning should be followed by etching with fine wet-and-dry abrasive paper before putting on gloss finish direct. Lead is poisonous, so wear gloves, use a mineral turpentine substitute as a lubricant for your abrasive, and rub off slurry with a rag, which you should dispose of safely.

Iron fittings
Iron pipes are rare, this metal being more commonly encountered in support brackets, grilles and gratings, and fireplaces. Where you find rust, it is no longer necessary to chisel, brush or scrape back to bare metal to ensure that your paint will stay put. After wire-brushing any loose rust away (a messy job rather than hard), you can choose between one of the jelly rust removers and those which can be painted straight on to firm rust, thus forming a chemical coating that can corrode no further. (Kurust is one example of this type of rust remover.) Once this is dry, any other paint can safely be used.

If the rust is so thick that it needs drastic action to remove it, or at least to thin it down to manageable proportions, there are several methods open to you. The most difficult will be wire brushing by hand—wire brushing with the aid of a power drill is much easier. Or you could use one of the jelly rust removers, or try scouring with steel wool.

For hole-and-corner work with a power tool you may need small cone-ended brushes (sold for de-carbonizing car engines) as well as the standard cup type. If you use jelly remember that it is very caustic, and if you choose the steel wool method use thin oil or parafin as a lubricant, removing oily traces with a mineral turpentine substitute before painting.

However you get rid of the rust, prime the bare metal as soon after de-rusting as possible.

Fireplaces are the only iron items likely to be found both unpainted and rust-free. Abrasion is not likely to do much good, except possibly to soften odd burrs on mantel edges, but after normal pre-paint cleaning, you should use a chromate primer, after which anything goes. Some iron fireplaces are quite ornate castings and respond well to metallic paints. The aerosols are especially useful for deeply indented patterns, which otherwise need painstaking work with a soft brush. Artists may like to pick out some parts of the design with second or third colours, but successful masking is not often feasible.

Radiators
Central heating radiators should ideally be de-mounted when you decorate. This involves shutting off flow and return valves, draining out the water and lifting the panel away from its brackets. Domestic scouring pads clean out the flutes easily, after which normal washing down is all they need. You should prime chips and treat any embryo rust patches, since they are potential leaks. Paint or paper the wall behind, not forgetting the brackets, paint the back of the radiator so that you can put it back as soon as that is dry, finally painting the front in situ, either before or after refilling.

Grilles
Hot-air grilles can simply be washed and painted, but often they suffer from accumulations of dirt and dust which can only be got at if they are de-mounted. Unscrew from the wall, collect dust, wash thoroughly, paint the back. When that is dry, oil the works, usually some form of shutter, screw back into place, and make good the damage which may have been done to the wall on removing the grille. Paint the front. Cellulose filler is good to use for any patching up.

MAKING HARMONY A FEATURE

It is not only those who are fussy decorators who may want to echo some of the main areas of colour in a room by using smaller amounts of them on parts isolated from the principal blocks. Few people ever find themselves in the happy position of starting with a starkly empty room, able to plan colours, textures, patterns, fittings and furniture entirely to their personal whim. Most people find themselves stuck with some piece of furniture, perhaps built-in, perhaps a part of furnished accommodation. Curtains or carpets can present this problem, even pianos if they do not happen to be black ones.

To take no notice of strong-charactered fixtures and to plan every other feature as if they did not exist may be courageous, but the results of such action will spell undiscerning obduracy to the beholder. If the nuisance is paintable, or if it can be covered with wallpaper (see pages 56-57) you have an easy way out of your difficulty. However, assuming that you can do neither of these things for some reason, there are two alternative courses open to you.

Featuring
You can adopt the pessimistic attitude of can't-get-rid-of-it-so-might-as-well-make-a-feature-of-it and leave it in splendid isolation, planning the other decor so it does not oppose it too strongly. There is no need to avoid contrasting complementary shades in such a scheme, of course, and you can also soften the fixed object's sore-thumb prominence considerably by painting other parts of the room to match it. Other parts need not mean doors or walls, although you could pick out parts of them. Try painting a window-sill, or the stretcher-rails of wooden furniture, or the picture or dado-rails.

Toning-in
Where your problem is the lesser one of a natural wood or veneered piece of furniture which is quite attractive in itself but the only thing of its kind in the room, paint will not solve it. You could in these circumstances either

add other pieces of very similar colour, put up veneered chipboard shelves sufficiently near in shade and character to make an effective echo, or, if you have a dado-rail, put veneered plywood panelling on the dado itself (the stretch of wall between the rail and the top of the skirting board). Although very warm and beautiful, this wood panelling is a fairly costly wall covering, but it need not be installed all the way around the room. One short wall could well be all you need to make the point.

Fixing panels

Although it is sometimes possible to stick the board in place with impact adhesive, few walls are flat enough to make for total success. Ideally, thin softwood framework should be screwed to the wall first, with the object of providing an even support for the plywood, which is only about $\frac{1}{4}$ in. (6mm) thick. With a short stretch of wall like a dado, it should not be necessary to go to greater lengths than to fix a vertical batten every 18 in. (.457m) or so, but each one does need to be made vertical with the aid of a spirit-level. If the wall is very uneven, try packing out the battens at top or bottom (cigarette packets are marvellous for this purpose).

The plywood itself can be sawn quite normally, with the common-sense precautions of cutting through the veneer with a craft-knife along your guide lines (so that the fine surface will not come away at the edges) and supporting the plywood underneath when you saw. Keep the support fairly close to your guide line.

Special, small-headed nails are normally used to fix the panels to the battens. If these prove insufficiently invisible when tapped flush to the surface, punch them slightly below it and fill in the holes with a wood stopping compound (e.g. Brummer) of the appropriate colour. As when you have any oblong area to fill completely with multiple panels, start fitting slightly less than one panel width from a corner, not in it. Corners are so very rarely as square or as vertical as they look, and it is so much easier to measure into them from a true line than out from them to make one.

Never try to remove picture or dado rails, unless you are prepared to put up with steps in the plaster, which was most likely put on after the rails were.

Painting furniture

Remember if you decide to paint the stretcher rails between the legs of chairs, settees or sideboards that they may perhaps have been wax polished. Scraping off the old finish is likely to be necessary, followed by scrubbing with fine steel wool and a mineral turpentine substitute. If there is no wax on them, normal pre-paint cleaning will do. Do not attempt such work on furniture which may be valuable.

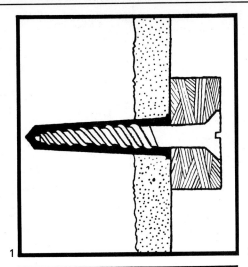
1

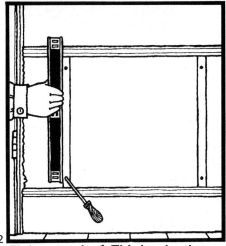
2

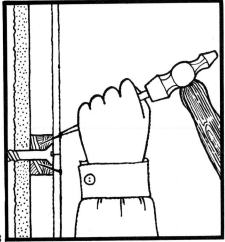
3

4

14 Opposite top: Clever co-ordination brings interest to a compact hall-way, where muted browns are accented by the clear red of the storage area, the flowers and jars. To bring down the ceiling height for storage space makes good sense here.

15 Opposite bottom: The hard line of the chair rail has been softened, and intriguing interest added, by using a border in combination with toning shades of green. The keyed-in plant and stand bring a final touch of harmony to an otherwise awkward area.

Fixing panels. *1.* This is why the top of an ordinary woodscrew is not threaded. All it does to the batten is pull, although you are twisting it to make its threads do that. The plaster is not strong enough to hold a screw, even with a plastic plug in it, so use screws long enough to penetrate at least an inch into the brick, stone or block behind. *2.* Put the top screw in before you drill the wall for the lower ones. With the batten swinging freely, you can use a spirit level to get it vertical, then hold it firmly while you mark the other screw positions. If the plaster is very hard, you may need a helper to hold the batten while you use a hammer and an old screwdriver to indent marks for the holes. Swing the batten aside while you drill and plug. *3.* Leave nail heads just proud of the panel, so that you can hammer them neatly into the board with a punch. Knock them a little under the surface, so that you can fill the little holes with coloured stopping and make them invisible. Angling the nails like this gives them better grip. The joins are pulled more closely together than if the nails were knocked in straight. *4.* The edge of each panel comes just half way across a batten. Always leave less than a complete panel width at the finishing or starting point. 'Starting point' is a bit of a misnomer, because you do not in fact start at the end of a flank, but at the first batten along. Fitting the part-panel completing pieces by this method gives you at least one guide to work from: an absolutely vertical edge. Measure and calculate the other sides of the part-panel from that and you will not be far out. It may be advisable to stick the end batten with impact adhesive instead of screwing it because there are often electric cables running inside door architraves, or near them. An all-plaster corner, however, should be safe to drill and screw into.

NATURAL WOOD STAINS

The suggestion of wood-staining may fall on present-day ears like something they might have done to the Ark, or a process which went out at the very latest with crinolines and candle-snuffers. Now that natural wood, however, has begun to be so much scarcer and more expensive than it used to be, and houses have become relatively featureless and boxy, there is a widespread resurgence of feeling for wood's colour and warmth.

Preparation techniques

Natural timber is just that: slices sawn off a tree, and as different from each other as successive slices from the same loaf of bread. Even new things made from new wood may have one part varying appreciably in colour from the rest. Provided that they are made by a competent joiner (professional or amateur) or a reputable firm, the shade variations between one component and another should be slight enough to be eliminated by putting wood-coloured stain straight on to the entire piece with no more preparation than smoothing.

It is always a wise precaution to wipe wood over lightly with a mineral turpentine substitute or methylated spirits, to make sure that the surface is not greasy. For the very best results you should wet the surface after the first sanding. This will raise the grain, which you sand flat again when it is dry.

Although this may appear to be a mindless rigmarole to go through, it does have a useful purpose. Stains tend to raise wood grain anyway, and raising the grain to flatten it before you use a stain foils this little action and leaves your wood smooth, without ridges.

Sanding

The first sanding, by the way, should be done with medium-grade woodwork glasspaper, about 100-grit, and the second with fine, about 150-grit. There are quite a few kinds and qualities, and perhaps the only type worth singling out for this purpose is one which incorporates a soapy substance to make it slide more easily (e.g. Lubrisil). It is particularly good at flattening softwood grain.

Restoring

In the days when all kinds of wood were cheap and plentiful, much household woodwork was made from timbers which today would command a high price for its beauty of grain. Indeed, some once commonplace have become well-nigh unobtainable. Douglas fir is a prime example of beauty which you are likely to find concealed under coats of paint, since it was widely used for doors at one time.

To establish whether or not a door is worth restoring, clean up a bit of the top with medium to fine glasspaper.

Wet the cleaned bit with water so that you can see what it would look like when sealed and then decide whether or not it is likely to look so appealing that you can think of the hard work of stripping the whole door as a labour of love.

Stripping

Chemical stripping is probably easier than burning-off for most people. Certainly it is the better method of the two if you do not want to redecorate everything else in the room at the same time. It does, however, have the disadvantage of leaving residues in the wood which you must carefully wash out very thoroughly.

Burning-off

Burning-off with a modern bottled-gas blowlamp is a technique easy to acquire. After paint has been taken off by so-called burning, sanding smooth is all you need to do before refinishing. What you do is to melt the paint, not burn it, although you will create the odd flare of flame now and again. Think of your torch-flame as softening and lifting the skin of paint. Warm a small area at a time, then point your flame into space while you gently scrape the wood clean. Never go back and scorch to dislodge obstinate spots; use very coarse abrasive paper (around 60 grit) instead. Burning happens when you leave the flame stationary, so keep it steadily moving. For fiddly mouldings which do not respond to your scraper, use a wire brush.

Old paint is one thing, but old varnish is quite another: discourage yourself from warming it.

Sealing stains

Before you choose your stain, make sure that what you are sealing it with does not object to anything that it is made of. (Read both tins.) See some actual wood finished with your chosen colour if you can, as catalogues can only approximate the shade. Old softwood is lovely in its own right, so choose a stain to bring out that loveliness, rather than to make it resemble oak or walnut.

Difficulties in applying stains are rarely encountered, as properly prepared wood soaks a stain up like blotting-paper. You need to be a little disciplined as to the degree to which you overlap one stroke on another, so if using a rag gives you streaks, try a soft brush or a paint pad. Always let a stain dry out totally before sealing.

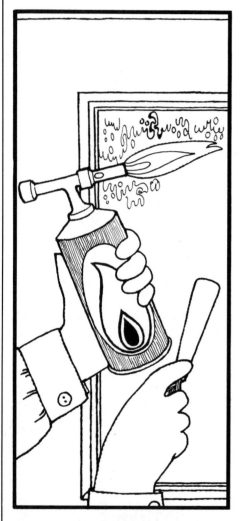

Use the blowtorch as if you were shaving the paint off with a cut-throat razor, rather than trying to drill a hole. When you have softened a small area, remove the heat while you scrape it clean. This is the most dangerous point of the operation, for you may forget what you are doing with the flame while you concentrate on the fascinating job of stripping. In the earliest stages of experience, you will inevitably acquire habits, so make sure the habit dictating what you do with the torch in between warms is a good one. Put it down safely or aim the flame into space.

16 Right: The warmth of natural wood can add softness and a relaxed comfort to a modern living area. Here, the ceiling's theme is continued down one wall, and emphasized by the special beaming.

Natural wood stains by their very nature aim to emphasize the warmth and richness of wood tones. But when colour and vividness are wanted in a room, the newer, coloured wood stains offer many possibilities.

17 Above: A study-office area is easily brightened up by using a coloured stain on the cabinets to match walls and accessories.

18 Right: Subtle shading can also be obtained when using coloured wood stains. Such toning works particularly well on single feature walls, such as can be seen in the right of this picture.

COLOURED STAINS

Not all softwood will have its appearance improved by the use of wood-coloured stains. If you have a chunk of uninspiring grain, possibly with a few knots in it, whose effect falls short of beautiful, encourage yourself to try a brighter coloured stain on it.

The effect of this treatment is far removed from what you get with the solidly opaque shades of paint, for (irrespective of depth or intensity) you will see the grain and figure of the timber. All coloured stains are semi-transparent, giving you added visual interest with the additional dimension of a random pattern.

Preparation—bleaching

Before you apply bright stains of any kind, it is almost essential to bleach the wood to ensure that you get a really uniform ground to work on, since shade variations which disappear under natural coloured stains may well have a much more marked effect on a brilliant hue.

Tempted though you may be to think of bleach as a plastic bottle of hypochlorite under the kitchen sink, resist the false economy and buy a proprietary wood bleach. Follow to the letter the instructions you get with it, particularly those about removing residues before you stain or seal.

Bleaches vary one from another as to chemical composition, but without exception they are most unkind to hands in the strengths used for whitening wood. Gloves protect you against skin irritation and ventilation against the fumes, if any. And if you have a cat, be nice, and lock him in the garage until the danger has passed.

Polyurethane varnishes

Half a dozen or so wood-colours and about the same number of bright pop-art hues can be had in the form of already-stained, translucent polyurethane varnishes. Any colour of a given brand can usually be mixed with any other shade of the same product to make intermediate colours. These seals offer you first-class protection for the wood, absolutely even colour (if granted an equally even surface) and save you time because they can be put straight on to the raw, prepared wood, so there is no waiting for a stain to dry. They all have a high gloss, however, so where you want a sheen-finish you will need to rub them down with very fine steel wool when they have hardened.

The colour of these stains may perhaps be more affected by the tone of the base wood than that of the stains themselves, but the more coats of coloured varnish you paint on, the deeper the colour becomes. Any seal or shine you apply to a simple stain just adds gloss, not colour.

Dyes on wood

As the range of shades you can get in stains made specifically for wood is severely limited, you may well feel a bit restricted, especially if you want to pick out panels, architraves or other parts of the area you are staining in a contrasting and original colour. Since certain types of fabric dyes (e.g. Dylon dyes), like many wood stains, are water-borne, they are perfectly compatible with most wood finishes and behave in much the same way as any water-plus-alcohol timber stain.

Apart from the enormously increased range of magnificent colours to which they offer access, they bring you great flexibility, allowing you to control the intensity of colours by altering the dilution at which you apply them. An essential extravagance is to mix more than enough of any batch to cover everything you want to be the same shade, as precise dilutions are difficult to repeat.

Preparation for dyes

Raise the grain of the wood in the usual way (see pages 20-21), using warm water fairly generously. Then flatten it: smooth to the fingertips rather than to the eye. It is only when you come to mix the dye that you move into the realms of adventure, as you need to experiment on scrap wood to be sure of the intensity your mixture will give.

Start with a small tin or jar and work towards a bucket. Mess about to your heart's content, but do remember that the dye also does a pretty good job on skin. You can put additional coats of dye on to previously well-dried ones to increase colour intensity, but once you have achieved an intense shade, it cannot be reduced, so if you want to play it safe, start with the bucket.

Colouring floors

Floors can be stained exactly as any other woodwork, provided that they are protected afterwards by the more resilient finishes. Special problems with floorboards make for some quite hard work, but the finished results are all the more rewarding. Few people expect a floor to be glamorous without a carpet, so the considerable element of surprise will add to the glory of your metamorphosis, and effectively prevent the inevitable footscars from destroying the illusion of grandeur.

The chances are that a floor in older property will have had severe wear in places such as doorways, and very much less under the carpets it has been hidden under. It will almost certainly have been cut into and repaired during maintenance operations on the labyrinth of service pipes and cables which are normally to be found beneath. As floors dry out over the years, they shrink and warp to some extent, producing an undulating surface difficult to sand. With further shrinkage, nailheads protrude and knots fall out. None of these difficulties is without solution, and are discussed more fully on pages 24-25.

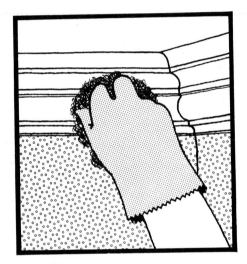

Whether you use heat or chemicals to soften old paint, if it happens to be flaking, dry and perished you may find stripping tools less than adequate for the obstinate residues. Steel wire wool is perhaps the best thing you can use in these circumstances. Like all other effective methods, rubbing with wire wool has its drawbacks. Even with a medium grade, the abrasive effect on the wood is relatively mild, but not so kind to your hands. Unless you have skin like chrome leather, wear strong gloves. Heavy duty rubber ones are good, but vinyl reinforced gardening gloves are probably the best.

WALK ON COLOUR-LACQUERED FLOORS

A floor is traditionally something to be covered up, a necessary firm, hard base for other smoother or more comfortable surfaces. It can, with a radical change of attitude be looked on instead as a new and influential vehicle for bright and dominant colour.

Types of floor lacquers

Most paint manufacturers include in their range finishes which are made specially for coating floors. They may be based on catalyzed lacquers, epoxy or polyurethane synthetic resins, or on combinations of any of these with alkyd media. The extent to which they will out-perform standard wood finishes in a domestic situation is marginal, and the dullness of the colours available may make you glad that this is so.

Some lucky people have open to them the greatest choice of solid-colour floor paints, because all their floorboards have never before been painted, varnished or waxed. Nailheads, joint gaps, knots and dirt are comparatively minor obstacles which most floors present you with, but some unlucky individuals will find themselves up against wax polish, ancient oil paint, brittle varnish—or all three.

If you balk at the prospect of removing inherited decoration, to give discriminating polyurethanes the uncontaminated base they need to produce their best form, you can still have a brilliantly glossy floor with the help of less demanding alkyd finishes. (Some of these contain polyurethane in some proportion.) Although their powers of endurance under extreme punishment falls short of what you might expect from pure polyurethanes properly treated, alkyds are far better-natured, very good mixers and will give you yeoman service for the minimum cost and trouble.

Preparation points

Like every other surface due for decoration in a room, a floor needs to be integrated into a thoughtfully ordered sequence of operations, based on your natural reluctance to spoil the results of work already done. When you go around punching nailheads below ground level in the floorboards, you will make the joists on which they rest bounce about, the joints between boards vibrate and change shape and the dust and cobwebs lying dormant in them to leap into prominence. It makes good sense to do the nails early on.

Dealing with gaps—using filler

Once the nailing is over, and creaks eliminated in the process, look at the gaps between floorboards and decide how to treat them. To ensure freedom from gaps, new boards are slotted into each other with tongues and grooves so that as they dry out they can shrink without parting company with each other. Gaps of $\frac{1}{8}$ inch or less can be disregarded, or filled with any proprietary filler, although an amorphous one which can be trowelled into the cracks and sanded flush on drying will give you a more continuous surface than putty-textured compounds. As long as you cannot see between boards to the spider's dungeon beneath, these fillers are perfectly adequate, but wherever open chasms have yawned, sterner measures have to be adopted.

Using softwood slivers

Gaps few in number or those fairly uniform in width may be bridged with cut-to-measure slivers of softwood. Establish the width of your widest crack and that of your narrowest one. The slivers you need should be approaching 1 in. (25.4mm) deep, not much wider than the narrowest crack at the bottom, but a little wider than the widest one at the top—extremely difficult to make by hand, but no trouble at all to a timber merchant. The amount to order is the total length of the crack needing to be filled plus 10 per cent for cutting, wastage and later repairs which may be necessary if the wires or pipes under the floor have to be reached for some reason.

Working in the longest lengths that you can, lay each sliver narrow side up alongside the crack it is to fill. Coat it fairly generously with a PVA woodworking adhesive, turn it wide side up, insert it into the gap and tap it firmly home with a hammer and a short length of wood. The glue will have set within two hours.

Finishing gap-filling

For alkyd painting you can simply level the protruding slivers with a kind of plane known as a Surform, but if you have decided to dig down to raw timber (for polyurethane), hire a machine sander so that you can level and de-varnish at the same time. This is quick, but it does make a bit of dust and mess despite its vacuum bag; hence its early place in the sequence. Before you give the sanded and repaired floor its pre-paint wash, however, prepare and decorate everything else so that the floor can be done last (painting towards the door) and not have to suffer stepladders being dragged over it.

Painting floors

Consider a mohair or foam roller for painting the floor, doing the edges first with a brush. Alkyds will perform best with one primer coat followed by two gloss coats, but polyurethane paints should go coat on coat. As the eggshell versions are as tough as their gloss ones, you have a choice of sheen or shine with them. No need to rub down between coats unless you allow more than a day's drying time. Always test before re-coating by scratching lightly with your fingernail: if it marks the paint, wait until a further scratch does not.

1

2

3

19 Above: A brilliantly glossy floor in a room with little furniture can be one way of giving the room a deliberately uncluttered look. Here, the reflected glow of the yellow lacquered floor shows off the lines of the bentwood rocking chair to advantage.

20 Right: Plan the colours of floors to offset those of walls and woodwork — add an extra spice of interest by painting a stencil border at floor edges.

1. Press the filler into cracks with a good sized trowel, using one long edge. Pat the little heap of filler into a flat slab, and cut neat, squarish section strips off it with the edge of the trowel which is going to put them in place. Do not forget that holes made by punching the nails down need filling as well. *2*. The piece of scrap wood you use to protect the infill beading when wedging it into the cracks need not be this shape. If you only have, say, an old floor-board, do not cut it up, but use it as it is. You may tread the beading in with such a board under your feet. *3*. Surforms angled across the line of push like this one cut more quickly. Straighten up for the final few strokes to avoid scoring the boards on either side.

FLOORS WITH A DECORATIVE TOUCH

21 Left: Painting each floor-board in a different tone of orange, brown or cream has brought this room to life, and has enhanced the appearance of its length and shape. The other colours in the room echo those used on the floor and create a delightful total atmosphere.

22 Below: In contrast, the cheerful splash and swirl of an all-over design has here created an uninhibited note, in combination with the pink wallpaint. Chocolate-brown sofas add strong contrast, and establish a downbeat of practicality.

Moving naturally along the path of adventure may possibly lead you to feel dissatisfaction with the concept of a floor as a single-colour, horizontal backdrop for people and possessions, and turn your thoughts towards ways of using extra colours to exploit your available floorspace. Whatever pattern or design you execute on it, you may be absolutely sure that it can never give an 'off-the-peg' impression. Every floor you paint is unique.

Colour points

To think of a second or third colour just for the sake of added brightness and contrast is to miss a golden opportunity of deliberately planning for a specific effect. Rooms can be made to expand or to shrink; to alter their proportions. You can reflect light into dark corners or employ darker shades to make a floor act as a dramatic foil for light walls or skirtings. Echo colours can be chosen, to integrate your floor into the total scheme of decor. Judiciously planned colour changes can delineate separate areas or cordon off particular zones.

Preparation

As if in compensation for being one of the most difficult surfaces to prepare for decoration, floors are one of the easiest to paint. All your brush and roller work is gravity-assisted; all paints are non-drip. Nevertheless, to ensure the best outcome of extra colour efforts, it pays to give careful attention to gap-filling (see pages 24-25 for details).

Where the gaps between boards are small enough not to bother filling for one-colour work, you might risk painting alternate boards in a second colour, freehand, having of course dug the first colour well into the joins. But for lines or patterns going across the boards, filled and smoothed gaps make for less trouble in painting, and a much better-looking finished masterpiece. In particular, you should fill and seal the space which shrinking skirting boards tend to leave between themselves and the floorboards.

Skirting boards

Before you do any filling, make sure the skirting board itself is not at all loose, because if it is the slightest knock may shake some of the filler out. Builders normally fix them in position with lost-head nails knocked through the boards into little wooden wedges which have been jammed into spaces left between bricks behind the board. Unless you have an exceptionally well-built house, you can usually tell where the nails are: you will see small dimples into which the stopping has sunk after the nails were punched invisibly into the wood. There may even be semi-circular indentations from the occasional mis-hit with a hammer.

Sometimes you can put matters right with an extra nail or two, but if the wedge has split you will need to take the whole board off to put in a new anchorage, or drill through the skirting and brick so that you can use masonry plugs and screws. Should the board be wobbly only at the bottom, the gap can be sealed and the board firmed at the same time by nailing quadrant-shaped beading into the angle.

Patterns in colour

Apart from painting alternate boards different colours, all additional-colour work needs assistance from masking tape (see pages 10-11). Since both alkyds and polyurethanes take longer to set hard than emulsions, and since you will most probably have put on thicker coats for the floor, you will need more than a little patience to avoid masking until previous coats are thoroughly dry.

Borders

Additional colour can provide you simply with a solid border, but a more interesting and economical-to-achieve peripheral interest is to paint a broad or narrow stripe some distance from the skirting board and parallel to it. Remember that your line should be geometrically accurate, no matter what contortions the surrounding woodwork may have got into. Taped designs can easily use geometric shapes to make semi-continuous running patterns around the edge of a room.

All-over designs

Perhaps you would rather deploy your extra colours to make all-over interest in forms like weave or check patterns, or to isolate certain areas. More dramatic impact can be gained by painting a single design out in the middle of the floor. Some national flag motifs make good copy for such devices.

Scale is a big consideration when you do insular patterns. Rules of thumb can always be broken if they do not work, but as good a rule as any to start planning with is: restrict your island-panel's sides to no more than a third of the length of the walls adjacent to them.

Floor stencils

Stencils can be made and used for floor decoration in similar fashion to those already suggested for walls. Alignment on floors may be a little more difficult, but juggling stencils about in order to get their positions right is easier, as you can put weights on them to hold the edges down. Metallic aerosols are quite appropriate for floor stencilling, of course, and especially useful for the people artistic enough to make stencils for heraldic designs.

Moving on to ideas for more bizarre configurations, using stencils or masking tape as appropriate, the field becomes virtually limitless. Diagonal stripes, zigzag patterns, rainbows, hieroglyphs, signs of the zodiac, crossword grids and star constellations are all within the bounds of possibility.

1. A quick way of producing patterns on the boards is to make simple criss-cross designs with masking tape, spraying contrasting colour over the resultant open lattice. Several light coats are better than one flooded one, as they are for a vertical surface. Not all aerosols are happy at being used horizontally, so you may have to stop frequently to clear the nozzle, unless you organize your masking so that you can spray at an angle without scattering colour where it is not wanted. Keep the spray moving constantly.
2. When the sprayed colour is bone dry, peel off the tapes in the reverse order to that in which you stuck them down. Pull at a sharp angle to avoid lifting any paint edges. If an end of tape proves difficult to dislodge, lever it up gently with a knife point instead of scrabbling at it with a fingernail. Used masking tape can be very messy, so be tidy with it.

1

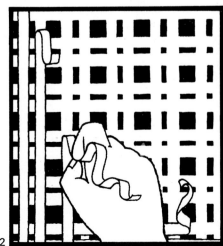

2

VARNISH-A TRANSPARENT PROTECTOR

As any good dictionary will tell you, the essence of a varnish is transparent protection, giving a hard, shiny glaze to whatever it is painted on. In the bad old days it frequently had to be used to finish outdoor paintwork. Then it was sticky, glutinous stuff, made from copal or shellac. It tended to dry brittle, and its surface crazed with age. The modern versions may be relied on not to do anything of the kind, being based on synthetic resins far superior to their tree and insect-derived forebears.

You can still buy traditional oily-resin varnishes, which are not at all as demanding as modern ones with regard to surface type or preparation, and which can do quite a reasonable job for you if all you want is a bit of a shine and ease of application.

The modern versions of varnish are based on oleo-resinous compounds, take little longer to dry than ordinary alkyd paints, and can usually be re-coated between 16 and 24 hours after you put them on. Most makes are lead-free, but do check that the can says so if it is important for you to have a non-poisonous finish—as it might be for painting a nursery, or a child's toy. Naked woodwork needs its first coat thinned with up to 10 per cent mineral turpentine substitute, followed by two further coats not thinned at all.

In places where abrasions and knocks are likely, or in which heat, condensation or liquid spillages are to be expected, the extra trouble of preparing for a higher performance finish will mean giving yourself less trouble in the long run.

Where varnish is appropriate

Unless you want to see something of the surface underneath a clear varnish, there is no point at all in putting it on. You can always find one of the opaque, coloured finishes to serve the purpose instead.

Starting from this premise, the sort of surface which might benefit from clear varnish will be obvious : attractive ones but vulnerable, and having no other finish on them to start with. Possibly stair treads would fall into this category,

or banister rails, or linoleum floorcoverings, or bright metal subject to tarnish or corrosion. Raw wood with an interesting grain or colour, perhaps a door or a floor, or even a softwood table top would be yet another possibility. A modern clear finish can make wood as resistant to heat, chemicals and abrasion as a plastic laminate.

Preparations

Solvents in synthetic resins have to be pretty potent. Most of them are likely to attack existing finishes and dash all hopes of successfully superimposing without stripping ; but they *may* not, so try a dab in an out-of-sight corner if you cannot bear the thought of taking the old stuff off. You just might be lucky.

Old varnish should be cleaned and rubbed down very thoroughly, to make a sound base for polyurethane or similar finishes. Rub with a wet-and-dry or a similar abrasive paper to give the necessary finely-etched surface, and then put on two coats of your chosen high-performance varnish, unthinned.

When you contemplate putting clear varnish on any surface at all, bear in mind that they all show up faults as efficiently as they enhance beauty, and that any foreign body left inadvertently on the work remains enshrined like an insect in amber.

Knots

At this stage, too, check any knots which are in the wood. Because these are actually slices of the central core of a tree or branch section, they may ooze resin, which can bleed through varnish or paint, or they may shrink loose or drop out. Filler is the medicine for looseness or disappearance ; use a coloured one if varnish is to follow. Before this goes on, coat the knots with a patent knotting solution. (Under opaque paint an aluminium-based primer is the better treatment; this is the most resin-proof one, and so the most effective for softwoods in general.)

Types of varnish

A clear varnish is not necessarily as

colourless as water, most being at least slightly tinged with brown. For almost every purpose they serve, this is an advantage rather than a drawback, but you may sometimes want glass-like clarity, and you are most likely to find it in a catalyzed lacquer.

Varnishes of this kind will only cure in the presence of a special chemical (usually an acid), although the catalyst chemical itself does not actually do anything in the reaction except stand and watch. Those varnishes easiest to use, then, are pre-catalyzed, coming to you in a single can with the acid already added. These you can treat pretty much as a paint, but do not brush unnecessarily once the varnish is evenly spread.

Some varnishes are supplied to you in two parts, one can containing varnish and the other the catalyzing solution on its own. All you do is to add the catalyst to the varnish, in the proportion advised by the maker (normally about 1 to 8), just before you use it. Once mixed, the solution is usable for only a few hours, so you need to be very accurate at estimating quantities if you mix a lot at a time. Catalyzed lacquers usually contain rather pungent solvents so open the windows before you start. Paradoxically, they do not like cold temperatures, either.

Both one and two-part lacquers may be based on any one of a dozen tough resins, all of them in the same league as polyurethane, and some based on polyurethane itself. Most of them are high-build products, so they may tend to sag on vertical surfaces and will need thinning to avoid the trouble. Very effective sealers, one coat can make a solid base for other decorative finishes.

As a rule, you get the choice of a glossy or a satin finish, but for a satisfactorily hard-wearing satin finish, say on a floor, it is advisable to use just one satin coat, on top of two glossy ones.

23 Right: Varnish may be used on metal to prevent tarnish or corrosion, and to seal in the shine. It is especially useful on door fittings which are exposed to the elements, such as this brass knocker.

24 Below: A wood-panelled kitchen is an obvious choice for a clear varnished finish — the beauty of the wood is protected from dirt and grease, yet displayed to its full advantage. A modern high-performance finish will give the best results, and protect against heat and condensation too.

SEALED-IN PROTECTION

Without any doubt, the day will come when you will be able to take for granted that wallpaper and fabric of all descriptions and qualities will be sold already processed for protection from its natural enemies. For the present, however, there is more than a sporting chance with more than a few wallcovering materials that posthanging precautions will be needed.

Types of papers
Vinyl-faced or other washable and soil-shrugging wallpapers are to be had in an increasing variety of patterns and textures, but the choice still falls a little short of endless. If you want a really cheap paper for a little-used room, or perhaps for lining a cupboard, a walk-in closet or the glory-hole under the stairs, or if you fall for one of the exquisite hand-blocked papers at the upper end of the price scale, you probably buy yourself a vulnerable surface with it.

The colours in vinyl wallpapers are carried by special PVC inks, heat-fused to their surface, so they become an integral part of it. Inks and dyes in absorbent paper surfaces, however, may well be as fragile and delicately adhering as the pollen on a butterfly's wing, particularly if they are metallic.

Newsprint and posters
Newspapers or theatre-style posters of sundry nationalities may be used wittily and with restraint in place of more conventional wall coverings. The two practical problems needing special care stem from the inherent flimsiness of newspaper and the consequent liability of the print to run when it gets wet.

Whether you use a standard wallpaper adhesive or a multi-purpose PVA adhesive, such as Clam 7, you should paint it on to the wall as thinly as possible (an ordinary paintbrush helps) and not on to the paper. To achieve the minimum creasing, use new papers if you can, and iron used ones beforehand. Roll each one on to a cylinder, as you might unbacked hessian, so that you can unroll it smoothly into position at your first and only attempt.

A PVA adhesive such as Clam 7 gives an immediate bond with paper, but the minimum of crinkling. It is very easy to secure flapping edges after the main body of the sheet is in place, but impossible to rectify mistakes made in the middle. Paste for one sheet at a time, as open time is very limited.

One advantage of using PVA adhesive is that it is very unlikely to prove incompatible with protective coatings for paper and fabric, such as Fend. Whatever the combination of paste and protection you choose, there will inevitably be a higher risk of minor trouble with these sophisticated wallcoverings than you would have with more conventional ones. It is a risk worth taking for the sheer originality of result obtainable.

Cleaning papers
If you choose to leave non-washable, absorbent papers in their original, unprotected state, you will ultimately have to replace or to clean them. They are most unlikely to react at all favourably to contact with anything watery, so you will have to look for some dry method.

One which works well for all but the most delicate papers consists of a large, spongy lump of rubber, very crumbly in character, which is used very similarly to a soft India rubber eraser. With this cleaner, it is best to go over a complete flank whenever you treat any specially dirty patches. Otherwise you will find that the cleaned area is appreciably lighter than its surroundings, and will consequently shout aloud not, 'I have just been cleaned,' but 'They left the rest filthy'.

Provided that you use the cleaning block regularly, before too much dirt has accumulated, your wall will proclaim that it never gets really dirty. On lightly soiled paper, the block is by no means hard to use.

Liquid cleaners with an extremely mild action are the alternatives to the physical cleaner. Even these can upset the more sensitive patterns, so try out reactions on an inconspicuous corner before plunging ahead on the full flank.

Seals for papers
Instead of frequent cleaning, you can treat wallpaper with a clear sealing solution (one of the best known proprietary brands is Fend). This is a PVA emulsion formulated specifically for protecting wallpaper, and about as near to a panacea for the soiling problem as you can reasonably expect. A trial-patch test is still advisable before wholesale application is embarked on. There are a few colours which may run, and some metallic or lustre effects which may change their looks a bit.

Papers which react adversely to Fend are in the minority, so if your try-it-and-see patch looks a mess and you know the pattern is not all that extraordinary, read the instructions. Like any other special-purpose chemical product, the sealer has its peculiarities.

It does not pretend to be a cleaner, so the best time to apply it is immediately after the paper has dried off after hanging. Of course, you can put it on to paper that has been hung for some little time, but you would be well advised to clean and de-grease the surface beforehand. Application should be fairly liberal, but very even, without more brushing than is strictly essential. Guard against runs as against the plague. On some papers they may produce stains.

Spraying
Fend will go through a spraygun, suitably thinned with water, suitably meaning just thin enough to go through the nozzle without gumming it up. Sprayguns vary, so the hard-and-fast rule is : experiment where it does not show until you get it right. A paint-roller can also be used to apply Fend, but not on embossed papers.

Once dry, the seal is highly water-resistant, most marks which get on to it being amenable to gentle sponging with a damp cloth. Vigorous rubbing and hard scrubbing are taboo. Ink stains can be intractable unless you can give them the damp-cloth treatment as soon as they arrive. Even then, traces may remain. If you let them dry, they will lose all solubility and become indelibly part of the scenery.

In addition to making the paper water and stain resistant, the matt and invisible coating naturally makes it reluctant to come off the wall when you want to change it. To get it off cleanly, any of the proprietary wallpaper removing compounds can be used.

Fabrics
Even the makers do not recommend Fend for sealing fabrics, and you are unlikely to find a slap-on or spray-on product that is suitable for this job. Fabric processing is really a factory prerogative. Even if you could get (say) a plasticizing sealer, you might find that it was not altogether compatible with one or other of the many other chemicals probably applied while the cloth was being manufactured.

If you are lucky, you might find a processing firm willing and able to apply the sort of stablizing or proofing treatment you want to unbacked fabric in small lots, but generally speaking you will have to take pot-luck.

Much of the distortion you might want to guard against by sealing could be avoided by mounting without adhesives, see pages 54-55.

25 Above: A relatively inexpensive and delightfully pretty paper is used here for lining shelves, to carry the wall covering through for a total effect. Sealing will protect the shelves' surfaces from careless or grimy hands.

26 Right: A truly unconventional approach to design ideas needs to be followed through with care. Here newspapers from around the world have been used to cover the walls, and have then been sealed to protect the flimsy and vulnerable surface.

27 Left : A patchwork of odd tiles, collected from a variety of sources, look enchanting grouped around a particular area or work surface. And whether you group by colour tones or merely make a random mix of tiles, their very differences will create endless interest and opportunities for discussion.

28 Below : Mirror tiles can make a particularly charming dressing-table backdrop when several different sizes of tile are used. Here, the large central one will provide an undistorted image for making-up ; the others add a pleasing and imaginative design.

SPECIAL EFFECTS WITH TILES

Tiles are a time-honoured institution, long valued for their permanence and their resistance to water. It is a great pity that their very usefulness has earned them such an over-large utility label, which tends to inhibit people from using them in situations other than the bathroom or kitchen. Technically, they are extremely versatile, in the sense that they can be easily stuck to any flat surface, no matter what its composition.

You are by no means confined to shining squares of bright colour, since the range made today incorporates almost limitless varieties of texture and design. All the same, tiles, once put on, are likely to be lived with for far longer than any other form of wall decor, so have a long, hard look before you decide which kind to commit yourself to. This way you will be able to constantly to congratulate yourself on having a beautiful, maintenance-free wall, rather than a bald acre of boredom that can only be changed with great difficulty.

Using tiles effectively
While it would be ridiculous to ban tiles from utility situations, it is less than reasonable never to consider putting them in other places, where their intrinsic qualities might be equally useful. Table and shelf tops are obvious candidates for the treatment, as are window sills and reveals, hatches and their little architraves. And what about hallways, many of them so awkward to reach that decoration once in a lifetime is enough? Porches and friezes might also be hot candidates.

Mirror tiles
Mirror tiles can make a valuable contribution to the overall effect of tiled surfaces, but they are better used as *trompe l'oeil* (optical illusion) devices to increase the apparent size of living spaces. Used as mirrors proper, they can give an impression of having been second-choice substitutes, because the total image is somewhat broken up. This very feature is, of course, part of their charm, if they are placed imaginatively.

It is often necessary, particularly in bathrooms, to put a mirror panel on a wall, where it must be surrounded by tiles. If you possibly can, get a panel whose sides are exact multiples of those of your tile units, so that you can leave a fitting-space without bothering to cut tiles. This is much easier than screwing a mirror of unplanned size to the wall and tiling up to it.

Fixing techniques
Before the advent of the do-it-yourself era, tiles had to be set in fine cement, with professional skill, but now even the professionals cannot always afford the man-hours needed for that method, and gratefully borrow the amateur's flexible adhesive. There are two extremely simple tile systems, one based on $4\frac{1}{4}$ in. (108mm) square tiles which are stuck on individually, and the other consisting of square sheets of strong netting which have small, mosaic-style tiles already fixed to them in a predetermined design. Sometimes these panels, usually about 10 or 11 in. (279mm) square, have self-adhesive backs.

Edging
With either type, quantity estimates are no trouble at all, but you will have to allow for special edge-tiles if you are planning for individual squares. Places to which tiles are fixed are as unlikely to be vertical or square-cornered as any others, so you never plan on being able to work from an angle.

To make a really well-ordered impression, put your base line just less than a single tile away from whatever you have to meet up with at the bottom. Lightly nail a slat of wood horizontally on that line, and use it to support the first row. Good sideways alignment involves centering the number of complete tiles which the surface will accommodate and cutting tiles to fit the smaller spaces on either side.

As ceramic tiles consist of a glass-hard, thin glaze backed by relatively soft clay, they have to be cut by scoring right through the glaze and breaking the backing along that line. If you find this difficult using a standard cutter, there are special cutters on the market which make the job easy.

Once you have fixed the tiles, with adhesive that suits the surface they go on, the decor is completed by rubbing white grouting cement into the spaces between the tiles.

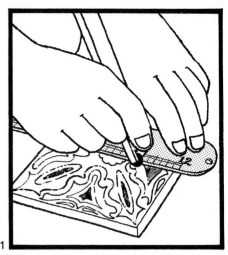

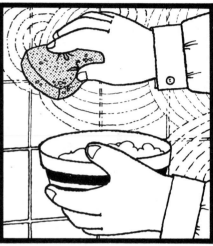

1. **Some tile-cutting tools have small tungsten carbide wheels, others have a brazed tip of the same exceedingly hard metal. Whichever kind you choose bear in mind that they do not cut the tile, but score through the thin glaze so that the ceramic body of the tile can be broken along the scored line. Place your straightedge so** that the scoring point or wheel is on the line. The guide rule may need to be some distance away. *2.* **Grouting is a very easy and pleasantly messy job. Most grouting compounds are cement-based, so wear old clothes. You may also like to wear rubber gloves. Do not wash the surplus cement off the tiles until that in the interstices has well and truly set. A damp sponge is the thing to clean off the tiles after grouting, not floods of water.** *3.* **Mirror tiles can provide unusually interesting effects in window recesses. If the adhesive does not give enough help with alignment, level up with cellulose filler before laying.**

CREATING SURFACE INTEREST WITH TILES

Of all the materials man makes use of, metals are the ones most peculiar to his purposeful, ingenious nature. Beavers build with wood, ants manufacture their own paper, a great many insect species produce resinous coatings or waxes, even dyes, but without man there would be no metal. Its magical gleam, imprisoned in the earth's rocks for so many millions of years, speaks to him of mastery over his environment, of armour and alchemy, of rewards and of riches.

Much of the special appeal which metals hold lies in their essential malleability—the obedience with which they conform to the countless different forms we shape them into. When metals are used decoratively this characteristic is exploited, mainly in order to bring out their talent for reflecting light.

Types of metal tiles

Gold for many years symbolized the sun and silver the moon, and these two metals still represent the extremes of warmth and of coldness available to us in terms of natural metallic colour. Since they are too rare, and therefore too expensive for purposes as utilitarian as decoration, their colours have to be imitated for us by alloys of baser metals such as copper and zinc. With these, almost any required degree of intermediate warmth or coldness can be provided.

Even base metals tend to be much more expensive than plastic or clay, so the metal tiles you can buy for domestic decor are almost invariably hollow. Most of them are manufactured by pressing small sheets of extremely thin alloy into a slightly dished form. From the front they look like solid plates of metal, a quarter of an inch or more thick, with the edges being bevelled or rounded as a rule to heighten this impression.

At the back they are correspondingly hollow, like little ashtrays. This feature is the most important practical difference between metal and solid ceramic or plastic tiles. It means that they cannot be stuck on to a wall or table-top in quite the same way. Furthermore, being non-porous, metals have always been notoriously difficult to stick. Special care is necessary even with modern adhesives.

Adhesion

Most manufacturers resort to using five small, self-adhesive pads on the back of each tile. These are thick enough to compensate for minor surface undulations and faults, so you will have no greater worries on that score than you would have with solid tiles. However, the adhesive used is normally an impact type which bonds instantly on contact, meaning that you cannot slide tiles into position. For this reason, metal tiles do not have spacing lugs on their edges, butting accurately up to each other, and they do not need grouting. You do, of course, need to be that little bit more recollected when you position your first row, but after that alignment is automatic.

Cutting

Except for stainless steel tiles, which may demand the use of a hacksaw, most metal tiles are made thin enough to cut very easily with ordinary scissors. Some metallic-surfaced tiles are, however, plastic plates which have been electro-plated. As the plating depends on electrostatic attraction for its bond to the plastic, it is as well to avoid cutting them if they are to go in heavy-duty situations such as kitchens or bathrooms.

Aluminium

Aluminium is a metal which lends itself particularly well to tiling. In brushed form it emulates stainless steel; in polished form it does duty as a mirror. It can be etched either pictorially or pattern-wise, or anodized (dyed) to provide a great variety of metallic colour. Aluminium tiles have the additional property of flexibility, allowing them to be bent around outside corners without any great trouble.

Polystyrene

Polystyrene tiles are different in character from either metal or ceramic ones, and there are two distinct kinds of polystyrene tiles different from each other.

Those which look like frozen soapsuds are, in fact, collections of plastic bubbles, trapping air. They are light, but as easy to damage as they are to handle. Special hot-wire portable machines are available to cut them with, although this is quite easy to do with a sharp craft-knife. The convex blades probably give the cleanest cut, used with light, scoring strokes.

Many standard adhesives have solvents in them which attack polystyrene, so use one of the special emulsion glues (e.g. Clam 24). You can spread it on the tile like butter, or use a splodge at each corner and another in the centre. Either way, do not try to press the tile into place with your finger ends. The flat of your hand is better, and a flat board, the same size and shape as the tile, is better still.

If you are leaving the bevelled edges on view, fill any unplanned gaps with cellulose filler before you paint: with emulsion paint, not with alkyd-based paint because that might have a solvent unfriendly to the tiles.

Solid polystyrene tiles look like ceramic ones, but they have a less glossy surface as a rule. Although the shine is less hard than a ceramic glaze, it is nevertheless attractive, and it does not provoke condensation. The same precautions recommended for the expanded polystyrene tiles discussed above, apply to these solid tiles. Adhesives are special (e.g. Clam 2) and painting (if you must) should be done with a gloss-finish emulsion paint.

1. **By far the neatest and quickest way of cutting expanded polystyrene sheet. The wire is electrically heated and melts the polystyrene as you push it along without danger or fumes. If the sheet is kept in close contact with the platen, you can rely on a sharp, clean and square edge to the shape you are cutting. This is why professional signwriters use this machine for executing exhibition lettering on the spot.**

2. **Ordinary household scissors will cut most tiles, but for stainless steel ones the additional leverage and harder heavier-section blades of tinsmiths' snips may be necessary. Even thin stainless steel will quickly turn up the edge of any tool you use to cut it, so start with a sharp one. All metal tiles rely on their press-bent folds for their rigidity. Once you cut away some part, much of the stiffness must go with it, so treat cut portions gently.**

29 Right: Work areas are just that much more pleasant to be in if one takes a little time to plan them for both attractiveness and practicality. Stainless steel tiles, simple to apply, have been positioned behind this workshef as a splashback — an excellent combination of colour and serviceability.

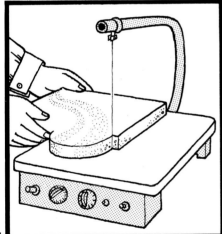

1

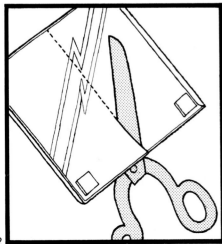

2

SEE-THROUGH DECORATION

Techniques

Glass is very smooth and flat. and totally non-absorbent, so there is nothing to be gained and everything to be lost by abrading its surface. Provided you clean all dirt and grease from it, glass takes paint as easily as any other material. One other important difference, however is that, since no paint will soak into the surface, the film of paint builds up thicker for a given applied quantity than would be the case with wood or plaster bases. Runs are easier to produce, so paint as thinly as you can, making up for them if necessary by extra coats.

Preparation

When you are putting masking tape on to glass, clean the pane first with methylated spirit, which will effectively remove grease for you. It will also deal with another troublesome problem, that of condensation. Since methylated spirit has the power to combine with water, it will enable the water to evaporate with it. Do not forget that the droplets of moisture can reappear very quickly, so that if you are bedevilled by a condensation film, you may (almost literally) have to work with a rag soaked in methylated spirit in one hand and your paintbrush in the other.

Polyurethane paints and aerosol sprays could have distinct advantages over alkyd finishes for glass painting—polyurethanes by reason of their much tougher, more scratch-resistant surface, aerosols because of the extreme thinness of their film, not to mention their useful metallic colours.

Applications

Painted glass used as a shade for artificial lighting could be considered the most effective application of the technique, not perhaps quite so effective with tungsten sources, but supremely well-adapted to screening the shadowless light produced by fluorescent tubes. These can be very difficult to shield attractively by standard methods, most of which are depressingly utilitarian.

Tape

Aside from painting on glass, you might prefer to try decorating it with one of the many new coloured translucent tapes or art materials now available. You will need to experiment with their resistance to the ravages of condensation and their possible effects but some novel decorations can certainly be produced. Since the tapes vary in their degree of translucency, you can cut out shapes in different colours which create unusual light-patterns within a room. Admirers of stained glass or Victorian decorative glass can try their hand at imitating some of these effects with the tapes.

1. Glass cutting presents special hazards. An uneven bench can exert enough leverage to crack the sheet when weight is applied, so watch out for bumps. Score the chosen line with the aid of a wooden straightedge — less likely to slip out of line than steel. As you score, move your non-cutting hand down so that it is always near the cutter. If the cut does not look continuous, run over it again.
2. A thin slat under the scored edge should be enough to effect a clean break with minimal pressure. Professional glass workers usually wear thick leather wristbands, but heavy bandages will give adequate protection.

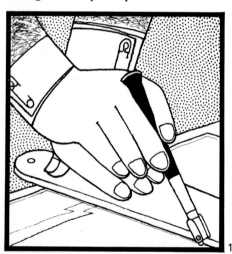

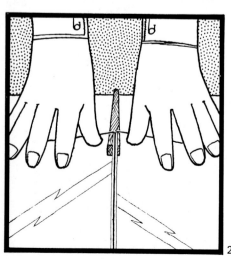

Although it may at first require a vigorous stretch of the imagination to think of painting and decorating on glass, the suggestion offers many attractive possibilities. To some people, the very nature of glass—with its primary property of permitting an unobstructed passage of light—seems to offer a hundred reasons for not painting it. However, this is taking a very restricted attitude to a material which offers numerous possibilities for enlivening home decoration. Many kinds of glass are meant to be seen through, but many others are meant to allow the passage of light without letting clear visual images through: stained and frosted glass are the prime examples.

No one is suggesting that you should set to with pot and brush to colour the lounge windows, but plain, clear glass in other situations can be treated to advantage. To paint frosted glass or stained panels is usually both a waste of time and an act of dubious taste. The possibilities to explore are concerned with the enhancement of smooth, flat, clear panes, perhaps in interior communicating doors or windows, perhaps in sheets of glass mounted as room dividers, or perhaps in smooth-edged pieces of plate glass hung purely to make a decorative point of interest.

Think of glass in these situations as translucent, rather than transparent. What you are trying to do when you put paint on it is to change the character of the light which passes through it, not necessarily to obstruct it to any marked degree. Unless the panel you are going to change can only be viewed from one side, you will have to paint both sides. Otherwise it will look odd from the unpainted side.

No great aesthetic good is likely to come of simply painting a glass panel all over with one, solid colour. The enhancement of translucency you are after is better achieved by painting intriguing patterns, random zones or picture outlines, leaving the rest clear. All the information in the pages about stencils and murals can be applied to glass panel painting, although there are some important points peculiar to glass.

It is not always possible to redecorate a room by applying new paint or paper to the walls. It is possible, however, to give a room a completely new look by applying novel decorations in restricted areas.

30 Right: This timber panelled bathroom has been given a special look by the addition of a cleverly decorated mirror. It is possible to achieve such effects by using masking tape, or stencils, and paint.

31 Below: Those who particularly appreciate the appearance of decorative glass can try using one of the many new coloured translucent tapes to create their own shapes and designs.

ADD WARMTH WITH CORK AND PINBOARD

Blackboards are by no means the only wall coverings applied chiefly for reasons other than the purely decorative. Lining papers are recruited to hide and to hold breaking surfaces, cork and some kinds of pressed fibreboard are employed to insulate against noise or heat losses, and other compressed sheet materials are used for temporary or permanent holding devices.

Pinboard

Pinboards (e.g. Sundeala) are fairly thin, fine-textured fibreboards with remarkable powers of self-recovery from drawing-pin wounds. Judiciously sited they can draw to themselves an enormously high proportion of the bayoneting suffered by the walls of children's rooms, or even by the back of the kitchen door. It is widely used for school and college notice boards, so you need have no fears for its resilience or longevity, but whether you turn it back to front or replace it at redecoration time, you will almost certainly want to take it off the wall or door to wash down, so screws are the most sensible fixing devices. Since its natural colour is pale brown, you will be glad that it accepts any kind of paint.

Perforated hardboard

Shops use on their merchandising stands and display boards a thin hardboard with regular perforations, usually $\frac{1}{8}$ in. (3.2mm) holes at $\frac{3}{4}$ in. (19.1 mm) intervals, which will accept standard wire hooks and other fittings. Many of these hardboards adapt themselves perfectly to household needs, and are far from difficult to get.

Hardboard with decorative holes does, however, need a little clear space at its back because the fittings must be inveigled into position, rather than simply pushed. This means pinning or sticking the panels of board to (say) half-inch square bits of wood at the edges before screwing it to the wall. Paint as you like.

Perforations in hardboard do not necessarily mean round holes, of course. Made from fine wood pulp, sheet hardboard is thin and dense. Since it is made by compressing a formless dough, indentations of many kinds are feasible, and it can easily be made double-sided.

In the literal sense, all hardboard is double-sided, but normally sheets have only one side smooth and hard, the back surface having been left uniformly crinkled to accept adhesives. Decorative forms having perforations in various patterns, however, are such natural choices for screen construction that they have to be made double-sided, smooth on both sides.

Some of the patterns available are very open, making the sheets suitable for duty as contrasting lattices through which more solid bases can be seen. Paint tends to squeeze off the brush into the perforations, so this is one of the few surfaces which benefits from skimpy coats, dabbed on with a well-scraped, soft brush.

Expanded polystyrene

Many insulation products make great use of trapped air. Cork does to a certain extent, but expanded polystyrene does to a remarkable extent—some two per cent of its weight consists of little plastic balloons and the rest consists of air, which does most of the insulating.

As far as wall cladding is concerned, expanded polystyrene is mostly used in $\frac{1}{2}$ in. (12.7mm) thick sheets of various sizes which are stuck by means of adhesive applied continuously or in blobs. In places where freedom from condensation is needed rather than significant reduction in heat losses, it is used in thin rolls, applied in a fashion very similar to that used for wallpaper.

Polystyrene surfaces are many and various, some usefully and attractively textured, others necessarily smooth, but all of them vulnerable. Knock damage is an obvious hazard, but there are a few less obvious ones. It is not more liable than any other wallcovering to be set alight, but it is readily flammable, and gives off poisonous fumes (phosgene) as it burns. Nonetheless, polystyrene is an extremely efficient and useful insula-

tor, and among the easiest to handle.

Special adhesives are absoutely necessary (e.g. Clam 143), as the ordinary contact adhesives you might be tempted to use dissolve the polystyrene. The adhesive itself may not like metal or plastics other than polystyrene. Even emulsion paint may upset it on occasion. Bear all this in mind, do not gloss-paint over polystyrene, and you are home and dry.

Cork

Cork has a beauty all its own, making it quite unthinkable to seal it with anything likely to obscure its comfortable brownness. The reason for putting cork on a wall is that it looks supremely warm and rich, rather than that it endows a surface with exceptional insulation. .To some people it may, then make more sense to use flexible cork, wallcovering than to fit tiles as you would on a floor.

Cork tiles

Tiles can, of course, be used to good effect on judiciously selected walls, or on parts of walls, for the purpose of increasing the tonal variety and surface interest. Thick and relatively inflexible tiles, however, need the most regular base you can give them: few walls will serve the purpose without at least some levelling work. The adhesive you use must suit both the tiles and the base, and above all else the base must be firm. Remove peeling paper or flaking paint, and seal whatever is left—loose plaster will be satisfactorily controlled by a binding primer, such as Leyland's Soucote.

Leave edges touching upon irregular corners straight, rather than trying to fit them to wandering contours. A slight unevenness where tiles meet can be levelled out by careful work with a block wrapped with medium glasspaper, followed by a fine grade. Sealing the finished tiles is very advisable; the best to use is a clear polyurethane varnish. Use two or three coats, and with all except the final, rub over with fine steel wool.

Flexible cork wallcovering

Hanging this is not much more difficult than hanging ordinary paper, but you will need to hang lining paper first, with the seams in the opposite direction to those of the cork wallcovering. Paste must be thick, preferably the boiling water type. Do not hang the cork until the paste has made it supple. Keep a particular lookout for cringing edges, sure signs that they would appreciate a further lick of paste. The surface, however, does not like paste at all, so quickly sponge off any that gets on it. Seal with polyurethane lacquer when dry.

32 Opposite: Use cork tiles to vary tone and pattern — here, with borders and contrasting wall sections.

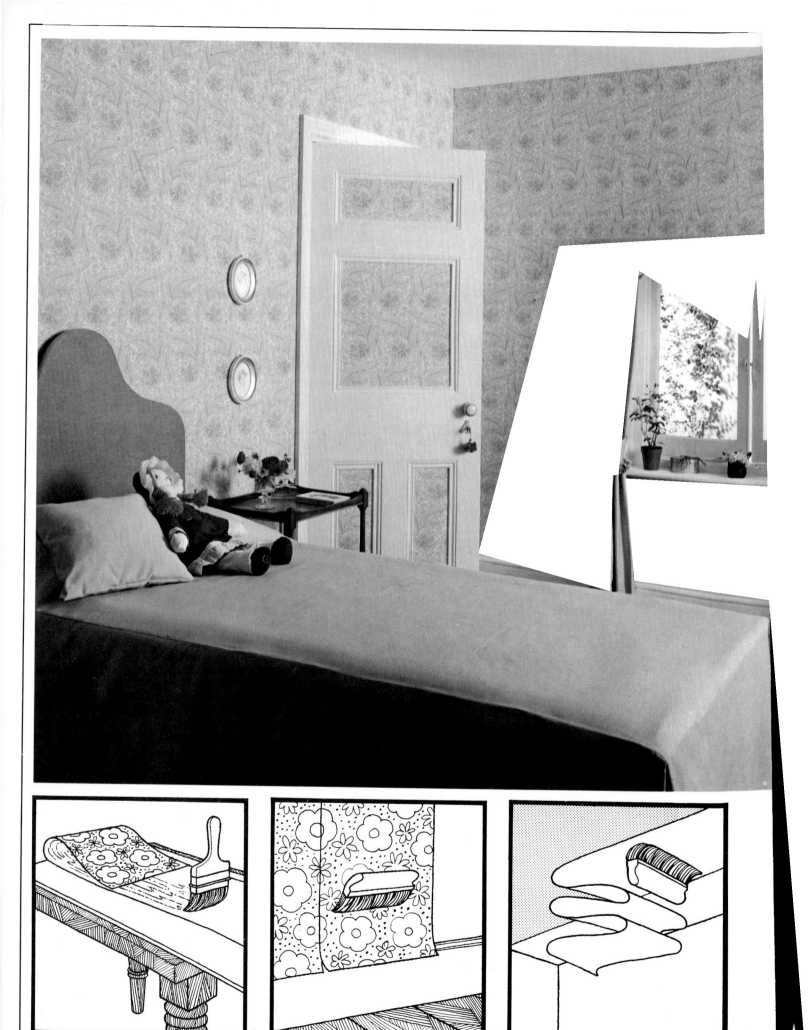

BASIC KNOW-HOW FOR PAPERS

Wallpaper can fulfil dreams or inspire nightmares with about equal facility. Perhaps more than any other decorating chore, wallpapering seems before you start to be fraught with insuperable dangers and difficulties. Half-remembered snatches of the old music-hall song, 'When Father Papered the Parlour,' float into your mind, accompanied by visions of yourself alone and helpless in the python-like grip of sticky and unmanageable yards of wet wallcovering. Yet, given reasonable preparation and a methodical approach, normal, non-specialist, modern papers and pastes make the process the easiest and quickest of the decorating projects.

Ignoring the special effect and textured wallpapers, about which more later, paper-throughout coverings can be broadly classified by weight. The lighter ones become flimsy when you wet them, so need to be hung as soon as the paste is on them. Medium

33 Left: A well-harmonized room, where paper has been used cleverly, integrating the door panels too.

1. Your pasting table need not be as long as your paper. As soon as you have pasted the first half, fold the end into the middle, then slide the piece up so that you can paste the other end. 2. Persuade the butt join to fit accurately before you brush the bottom fold to the wall. 3. This is how to fold pieces which are to go on the ceiling. Folds will not stay obligingly open like this, of course. They are opened out for clarity. 4. Unless you take courage and pull paper well away from the wall to trim the edge, you may tear it.

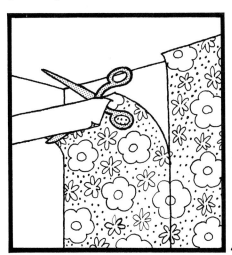

4

weights may need to be left pasted for a time until they are supple enough to do as you tell them. The really heavy ones like a longer paste soak. Treat most vinyls as medium weights.

Preparation

Paradoxically, wallpaper is the first consideration when you start to plan, but the very last decorating operation that you carry out. The reason for deciding on the type and pattern before anything else (quite apart from harmony problems) is that the wall or walls earmarked for paper need to be cleaned, filled and smoothed almost as thoroughly as for paint.

If the walls are freshly plastered, find out if lime was used to mix the plaster, and in that event give them a pre-paint wash (a good idea in any case) and a coat of alkali-resisting primer. Old paint also needs pre-painting treatment. Any wallpaper should be soaked or peeled off and the old adhesive paste washed off.

All walls, no matter what was on them, need to have holes and cracks filled in (use a cellulose filler such as Polyfilla), and the fillings and other miscellaneous bumps smoothed out with medium to fine abrasive paper.

You do not need to be half as fussy about smoothness as you do for painting, as long as you get rid of any grit, lumps and craters which can be felt as major obstacles to your hand.

You may find that gloss paint does not give much grip to the paste, so it should be etched slightly with glass-paper or an abrasive paint cleaner.

Measuring

Your stripped, cleaned, patched, and smoothed wall should now be covered with the same paste you are going to use for the paper, but diluted as the makers recommend for sizing, the trade name for the process. When that coat is dry, rub the wall fairly hard with your hand to see if any dust comes off the surface. Size again if it does, and again if need be until it does not.

Only at this point do you reach for the wallpaper. Having made things easy for yourself by choosing a pattern without a hypersensitive surface or a very big design-repeat gap, you will have been able to estimate how many rolls you want fairly easily.

Take as a sample size for a standard wallpaper roll, 33 ft. (10m) long by 20½ in. (520mm) wide. Measure the height of the space you have to wall-paper, add on 4 in. (101mm) for trimming, another few for the pattern

repeat if any, and see how many strips of that total length you will get out of a roll. Divide 20½ inches (or the width of your roll) into the total width of your wall, measuring as if the doors and windows were part of it. This gives you the number of pieces. If the pieces are 8 ft. (2.4m) long and the wall is 10 ft. (3m) wide, you will get six pieces on it (using our sample sizes). There will be four pieces in each roll (of our sample size), so you will have to buy two rolls. This will give you something to spare, which is better than not having enough.

Always check to see that all rolls for the same job have the same batch number, or colours may vary.

Hanging Paper

A kitchen table with a 6 ft. by 4 ft. sheet of hardboard resting on it will hold the sheets of wallpaper clear of the floor while you paste them, fairly generously, with a 6 in. (152.4mm) or larger brush. When you have pasted from the middle down to one end, fold that end into the sheet middle, pasted side inwards, so that you can paste the other half and do the same with that. It helps if you fold the top of the sheet further down than the centre, and the bottom not so far up.

Make a vertical line on the wall with a plumb and chalked string. Then use your forearm as a towel-rail over which the pasted sheet can hang, bottom fold away from you, and mount the step-ladder near the vertical line you have made on the wall. Pick up a corner of the top fold and peel it free so that you can slap the top edge on the wall.

Aim to leave two inches (50mm) or so above where you mean to trim the edge. Let the rest of the sheet drop gently down the wall and slide it about until its edge is in line with your plumbed mark. You have time to take the whole sheet off and reposition it if you need to. Leave it stuck but untrimmed at the top, come down the steps and gently pull the bottom fold free so it can be smoothed into place. Ease out bumps or wrinkles with a paperhanging brush, working from the centre outwards and towards the top and bottom.

At this point you can tuck the edges into rail, moulding, cove or skirting by drawing the scissors back gently along so as to crease the paper well into the contours it has to fit. Then pull it sufficiently clear to give yourself a clear view of the crease and slice off the waste. Smooth the paper back into position and wipe off spare adhesive.

Two buckets make for clean finishing: one for paste and one for clean water and sponge. All the remaining complete lengths go up in similar fashion, either following on from the first or from additional plumb-line marks where necessary. Corners and short bits are explained on pages 42-43.

COPING WITH PAPER ON PROBLEM AREAS

Invisibly butt-joined pieces of wallpaper have always looked far neater and intended-that-way than those overlapped, however neatly the overlapping has been carried out. Most manufacturers now thoughtfully machine-trim the edges of paper rolls so that edge-to-edge joining can be done relatively easily, even by inexperienced hangers. Even the most confident of paper hangers can, however, come across the occasional surface so uneven that overlapping is the only way to make it presentable, short of replastering. Overlapped joins are not in themselves difficult, but where they have to be made between sheets of vinyl wallpaper you may need a different adhesive from the one used to bond the paper backing to the wall. A multipurpose PVA product, such as Clam 7, is the kind to stick overlaps.

Vinyls
Vinyls are, of course, not porous to any great extent. They seal a surface so effectively that they create conditions very favourable to the development of any mould or fungus spores that may be invisibly hanging about behind them. As long as they are not visible the simple precaution of using a paste which incorporates a fungicide is the only one you need take.

Ready-pasted vinyls
Like many other widely used papers, vinyls are becoming increasingly available in ready-pasted form. You still need to size the surfaces you hang them on, especially if they are at all porous, but once this is done, the only remaining brushwork necessary is smoothing pieces into position.

Instead of a pasting table, use a small trough filled with clean, cold water. Some manufacturers will give you one free with each roomful of wallpaper. All you do is cut pieces to length, making the normal allowances for trimming and matching, and roll each one up fairly loosely (top edge outermost) so that it will unroll ready to hang.

You need have no fears about running out of slip; the only way to obtain dry patches is to leave the rolls in water too long. Position the trough close to the skirting, immediately under the patch of wall the paper is to go on. Dunk the roll smoothly in, one end slightly before the other so that no bubbles are trapped which might prevent the adhesive on the paper from absorbing water. Thirty seconds immersion is ample at average indoor temperatures, bearing in mind that much of the piece is under water for longer because you unroll it relatively slowly.

Of course, no folding takes place if the piece is to go on the wall, but you should have the step-ladder in position so that you can climb up to place the paper on to the wall straight out of the trough. From this point, you proceed exactly as for pasted-with-a-brush paper.

Odd areas
Hanging measured pieces of standard width paper is what covers most of the wall for you, but hanging the corner and end bits is what takes the time, together with fitting around projections of various shapes and sizes. Short sections over doorways and under windows are usually as simple to fit as the broad ones you started with, but leave them until all the parts needing longer lengths of paper have been covered.

Few corners are perfectly square or vertical, so plan joins to fall an inch or so from them, never precisely in them. If it's necessary to cut narrower widths than standard, cut them before you wet or paste the paper.

Fitting around switches and sockets
Electric switch and power points can be accommodated in the course of hanging, provided that the power is safely turned off at the main source and that the covers are modern ones, with screw-on top plates. The trick is to loosen these until they are half an inch or so clear of the wall before hanging the piece. Stick the top part of the paper's length, then cut two slits crossing where the obstruction's centre comes. These will be long enough to allow the plate to pass through, and once this stage is reached the paper can be stuck down behind the plate, trimmed closely so as to tuck just inside the plate's edges. When the rest of the length is smoothed down, the paper will be free from stress and the slits invisible.

Older electrical fittings may be mounted on circular wood blocks. These need to be planned for similarly to protruding pipes. Either set a join to coincide with the circle's middle, so that you can make semi-circular cuts, or mark the precise position of the required circle on dry paper and cut it out before pasting. It should be just a bit smaller than the projection and

short radial slits should be made around its perimeter so that it can be tucked neatly in place without tearing.

Stairwells
Papering on stairwells requires the same techniques, but has the added difficulties of access and height. The access problem must be resolved safely, either with firmly supported planks or with a hired sectional platform with jacks to support its feet. An accomplice in wait below is invaluable.

In default of a hired platform, use good, solid planks, well over an inch thick. Measure how far from the top trimming point of your wallpapering stint you need to have your walking planks, which should have a total width of at least 1 ft (305mm), and preferably 18 in. (458mm). Then measure the height of your upper reach-point above the highest bit of solid floor underneath it. This will usually be a landing or stair-turning. The chances are that this will not be high enough, so that a trestle or stout box will have to be put on it, to bring your walking-planks to a comfortable working height. Unless the area of the landing is generous and the support really jump-on-it stable, secure it temporarily but firmly with screws or nails.

As the stairs will fall away from the box-support, you will need a short ladder between them and an opposing wall to hold up the other end of the planks. Protect the wall by wrapping felt or other cushioning material around the ends of the ladder stanchions, and do not lean the ladder too steeply. If it even feels as if it might begin to lift away from the wall when you step on the bottom rung, move the foot of it up a step or two.

Look hard and long at the finished assembly before you trust your life to it. If there seems any possibility of any plank sliding on its support, cramp it, lash it or nail it down—use G-cramps, clothesline or four-inch nails.

Ceilings
For ceilings wallpaper must be folded into a series of short loops, rather like those of a jumping firecracker/traditional sea-monster/sea-serpent. The object of this is to defeat the force of gravity by allowing successive short foldfuls to be smoothed into place while the remainder of the piece is still manageably compact. Site the boards and trestles essential to the operation so that you can move from start to finish of a piece of wallpaper without stepping down. If one direction of working gives you shorter pieces to manage than the other, choose that direction. And do try to enlist the aid of a helper.

34 Right: A dismal attic has been transformed into a happy, sunny and comfortable child's bedroom through the clever use of paper on the heavy sloping ceiling.

1. When you cannot lift a switch plate to tuck the edges under make radial slits like this, snipping off the tongues as neatly as possible. 2. A typical staircase/landing setup. Note the cramps, the ladder-end protection for the wall and the screwed 'chock' for the stepladder.

35 Above: The large expansive feeling of this room is mainly a result of careful wallpaper planning. The graduated colour spectrum of the stripes has been positioned so that the darker tones begin close to the window, open up to cheerful yellows and reds where the wall has the greatest concentration of light, darken again in the corner, and finally open out on the wall opposite the window. The total appearance, against the essentially neutral furnishings, is one of fluidity and expansiveness.

36 Left: Often, striped wallpaper can be used very creatively by cutting out sections of the pattern to use as a frame. Where this is done, such as in the hallway shown here, an illusion of depth can be created.

PAPER IT STRIPED

Just as you pick horses for courses or pegs for holes, you sometimes have to choose wallpaper patterns according to the bases on which you are sticking them. If you are wise, you will take into account your own skill and experience, which build up incredibly quickly if you avoid trying difficult designs on awkward surfaces too soon. Nothing builds confidence like success: nothing destroys it more quickly than failure.

The knack of fitting paper around projections is easily acquired, but bulges, hollows and corners off-square or leaning severely out of the vertical present less tractable problems. Gauge your state of confidence before choosing your pattern, and if it's low, go for one that does not create additional worries: perhaps a small-repeat, all-over design or a plain, one-colour weave.

Matching joins

A good basic formula for bringing at least visual stability to uneven areas is to work in widths as narrow as may be necessary to spread the inevitable misalignment acceptably over a number of joins. The object in this situation is to leave no single join with a readily noticeable matching-error. On broad flanks you will most probably be able to get away with complete standard widths, the part-width device being needed mainly in and around corners.

Imperfect surfaces

Beware the thought that if you put on a sufficiently striking and unusual pattern (say, a rich-looking hand-print or French scenic design), no one will notice that the wall is askew. Psychologically you may well get away with it, provided that no one is allowed to look too close or too long. But technically hand-blocked papers are unlikely to have the surface toughness of machine-printed ones; so many have delicate inks or dyes on them which will not happily withstand even normal smoothing, let alone the extra pressing and tucking you may have to resort to on bad wall surfaces.

Striped patterns might at first thought seem to be the last to choose for untrue surfaces, but they can disguise faults extremely well. This may be because it is very difficult for the eye to rest on any particular spot on a striped surface, its natural tendency being to follow the lines to their extremities. Or it may be because the subtle shadows and contours by means of which our visual system detects an irregular surface are less obvious in the presence of strong superimposed stripes. In any case, human vision is a better judge than you may imagine as to whether lines are truly vertical or horizontal, so get the main body of stripes right and confine all juggling to the joins.

Special effects

Regular, evenly distributed stripes are the perfect medium for creating optical illusions. Broad ones can shrink vast wall expanses, narrow ones can add breadth to small spaces. The old rule of vertical stripes adding height, and horizontal ones adding width, in truth depends not on the stripes direction but upon their width and density.

Remembering this, you can of course employ horizontal ones to lengthen walls or to lower ceilings, and narrow ones to lend increased scope to tiny rooms, always depending on the nature of the stripes themselves. You add interest wherever you introduce them, whether you use their capacity for moving the eye along to camouflage irregularities, or to draw attention to special features. Perhaps you have a deeply set window, which not only distributes light inefficiently but gives a depressing, prison-cell feeling to the room? Colourful, narrow stripes on a light ground could be deployed to counteract both its shortcomings—running around all four flanks of the reveal thus making it appear less deep, and at the same time reflecting more light, of a more cheerful colour, into the interior.

Attics and other rooms with sloping ceilings offer unusual opportunities for imaginative exploitation of striped paper's versatility. Steeply sloping ceilings abound in challenges, and

their skylight or dormer windows give you dramatic variations of light intensity. Laid so as to radiate from a small window and stopping only at the nearest major obstruction, such as a roof beam, stripes can emphasize the presence of the obstruction and add materially to its importance in the total scheme. Threatening slopes may be tamed by horizontal stripes, if these are broad enough to reduce the scale of the slope and make the overhang promise you protection instead of doom.

The golden age of the stripe was undoubtedly the Regency period when it was intended to make a formal background for the graceful, solid and dignified furniture of the time, whose lines derived from ancient Rome. To use the more restrained and classic stripe designs is to borrow from an earlier epoch the stability and order of a more gracious time.

Wherever you take striped paper around a corner, whether an inside or outside kind, you will probably have to adopt this technique. The piece that actually turns the corner is not allowed to continue around it for more than 2 in. (50 mm). The following piece is hung with its leading edge plumb, so that any lack of parallelism goes where it is least likely to be noticed.

CREATE AN ILLUSION WITH TILE PAPER

Every wallpaper is intended to create some sort of illusion, and many are based on reproductions of real things so that their effect works well. Tiled paper, however, creates a very special effect, and to ensure that these papers will work in the way that they are intended, they must be used sensibly and with forethought.

In fact, it is because tile papers are supposed to look like 'the real thing' that problems may become apparent with layout. If real tiles were used instead of paper any faults or imperfections they contained would probably add to, rather than detract from, the finished result. But a papered tile must appear to be perfectly in keeping with the laws of possibility, and if the rules are not followed the finished result will be more likely to disturb the eye than please it: an incomplete or inaccurate illusion really will defeat the object completely.

This is the primary reason why you need to handle with some care wallpapers which purport to represent tile upon tile, each perfect in itself as well as in relation to its fellows. Everybody is going to know perfectly well that you have not suddenly acquired a supremely efficient tiling technique, but they will not mind being deceived, so long as you manage this efficiently. A conjurer who messes up a good trick can scarcely complain if his audience notices.

Tiles have always been thin, ceramic veneers, which were stuck firmly in regular and ordered ranks over essential but rather unattractive building materials. Since it was never completely possible to get rid of the joins, you openly admitted their existence and put them into some sort of order as well, so that they would not obtrude their presence any more than necessary.

Hanging tile papers

When you hang tile-pattern papers, then, keep constantly in mind what you can and cannot do to tiles. Cutting and hole-boring are totally legitimate operations, and you can cut out straight-sided notches at a pinch, even curved ones, but bending around corners is taboo. Good, flat walls provide the most helpful basis for tile effects, although gentle undulations will not completely invalidate the impression given by the finished flank. It's where the wall surface is interrupted that you need the most ingenuity and forethought.

Before starting, however, try to plan the disposition of the overall pattern as if it were a single sheet of paper. Measure or calculate the sideways repeat so that you can centre the design, leaving equal pieces of 'cut' tile at either extremity and remembering that even if a doorway comes at or near one end of a flank, the extremity is the wall corner, not the upright of the door's architrave : technically the doorway is an obstruction.

As regards positioning your horizontal tile-joins, you will be very lucky to find a rail, moulding or ceiling corner level and straight enough to allow a whole row of tile-joins to coincide with it. Try it if you think it will work, but keep one eye on interfering projections lower down the wall, especially those with curved edges. It may well be advisable to raise or lower the paper to arrange for the curved obstructions to centre themselves at a tile join, but at all costs leave more than half a tile-depth at the upper limit of the wall.

Matching at angles

Because real tiles cannot be bent, standard matching procedures may have to be abandoned in the angles and at the outside corners. The latter are best left out of tile-pattern plans altogether, as whatever their contours they are bound to kill any attempt at verisimilitude. If you must turn inside angles, you can do so without destroying the overall effect, but avoid angles entirely if possible. Cut your last piece of tile-paper so that it will just turn the corner, by about half an inch. Then make no attempt to continue the pattern from there, but start working in the reverse direction, from the chosen extremity, paying attention only to alignment of the horizontal joins, finishing by trimming the paper precisely to the line of the angle, so that 'cut' tiles meet other 'cut' tiles more or less naturally.

Large scale patterns

Analogous thinking needs to be applied to papers with large-scale patterns, most of which are loath to turn corners or to stop short part-way through a repeat. While it is always practicable to stop at angles, hori-

zontal cuts are inevitable. Once you have decided firmly whether cut repeats are less obtrusive at the top or at the bottom of the wall, start with a whole feature, and from that point onwards what is not forbidden will be compulsory and life will become gloriously simple to the end of the job. One advantage of large repeats, of course, is that obstructions can come anywhere at all without breaking the flow of the design.

Unusual uses

There is no need to think of tile-pattern wallpaper as a feature which must be used to duplicate the appearance of a regularly tiled wall space. Instead of covering an entire wall space, cut the pattern out to cover two-thirds of the height of a wall or to act as a border around a window, large pinboard, cabinet or whatever. Be imaginative.

If tile effect patterns are treated in corners as if the tiles were real instead of imaginary, their illusion is better maintained than if they are regarded simply as another design, and continued around the angle regardless. The technique is almost the same as that used for getting striped papers around corners, but the follow-on piece in this case is trimmed precisely to the angle. You can see here how the placing of an incomplete tile row at the skirting board edge maintains the reality of the design.

37 Below: Tile-pattern paper can sometimes be just as effective, and occasionally more practical, than natural materials. Compare the appearance of this bathroom, finished in cork-pattern paper with the bathroom finished in natural cork on page 38.

38 Right: The geo-metrical regularity of tile-patterned wallpaper makes it ideal to use for cut-out shapes. The breakfast nook seen here has been given an individual touch by carrying the paper two-thirds up the wall and finishing it off with a scalloped edge.

39 Left: The quality of marble-pattern wallpapers often surpasses that of real marble — and its general versatility cannot be compared with that of a heavy slab of stone. In the setting shown here, these inherent features have been put to use with quite elegant results. The triple-layered frame around the mantelplace has been made from strips of marble wallpaper.

40 Below: Metallic and foil wallpapers may need special care during their application, but the final appearance is totally unique. In this sitting room the foil-covered walls make a good background for pictures.

HANDLING SPECIAL EFFECT PAPERS

The vast majority of special-effect papers have designs which imitate something else, perhaps more expensive than wallpaper, perhaps more difficult to install in your home. Even those which represent nature in the abandon of high summer, or trees, grasses, flowers and less specific forms of herbage fall into this group. Similarly to tile papers, these equally imitative designs are expert in their execution of elaborate ruses, which are universally accepted as such.

Many are produced by photographic techniques which endow them with truly lifelike accuracy. Some are prepared by extremely talented artists who have the power to distil the essence of nature's charm and beauty, which they may stylize to a greater or lesser degree. Modern manufacturing technology is well-equipped to make the most of their efforts, so that the decorator is presented with a truly bewildering choice.

Choosing

A wide choice, however, is best regarded as an opportunity to get outstandingly good decor, rather than as an obstacle to its achievement. Having chosen the general effect you want, use the vast ranges of patterns available to obtain the design and the quality which suits your particular purpose.

Ruses with wallpaper need to be well executed if the jokes are not to fall uncomfortably flat, and executed with papers that are very well-made to start with. Modern methods can easily produce surfaces appropriate to the natural or hand-wrought material the wallpaper pattern is imitating, so if you come across one that does not look quite right in this respect, look on it as poor value for money and move on in your search for one that does ring true.

Marbled paper

Marble patterns are a very illustrative case in point here. Think of all the real marble you have seen in your lifetime and you will realize that it's always extremely smooth and extremely flat, and that (unless it's laid in the form of tiles) much of its charm lies in the unbrokenness of its random pattern lines.

Marble is, in fact, crystalline limestone, and crystal hardness, crystal smoothness, coolness and permanence are the impressions you try to recreate when you use a marble-pattern wallpaper. The manufacturer will already have outperformed nature for you, enabling you with a little care to stick on your wall a continuous slab of superlatively-marked, smoothly-polished stone that you probably could not even obtain for real, let alone afford.

Dealing with corners

Taboos on turning corners apply to marbles as they do to tiles. To get the most attractive possible effect from marbled paper, think of your wall as a single feature, one solid, splendid slab from your private quarry. Your other walls can be decorated with lesser materials to complement it.

To attain such an effect, you will need to take a little more than average trouble with matching and trimming, so as not to mar it with uncontinuing veins or kindergarten scissor-work at the edges. Treat yourself to a good pair of top quality wallpapering shears with heavy-section, precisely-set blades, so that you can cut clean, crisp, and straight. Take your time in aligning the meeting edges of adjacent pieces; work down the stepladder and coax them into agreement all the way down. Above all, reserve your flattest walls for the marble treatment.

Light-texture papers

Lightly textured papers do not need a great deal of special treatment to produce acceptably continuous surfaces, but cast a wary eye over the all-over basket-weave kinds which have often been given slight, regular variations of line or texture not apparent in small samples. Look at the helpful, whole-wall picture if there is one in the sample book. If there is not, lay a couple of rolls out side by side and check for recurring thicker, lighter or darker strands and similar matching indications. The maker may have put arrowhead marks on the backs of mating edges to show you where to join them.

Metallic papers

Metallic papers may well need special care. They may consist of metal foil, or metal plated on to plastic. Even the foil ones may have a thin, transparent plastic coating to ward off corrosion or discolouration. Always avoid heavy pressure on the surface, and take heed of any recommendations the maker may offer as to surface preparation and adhesives. Most of the metallic wallcoverings can be stuck with standard cellulose adhesives, but some of them are adversely affected by acidic solutions and may appreciate a bit of washing soda in the paste. Few of them can be rolled without damage, whether they are crinkled to start with or not.

Matching paper and fabrics

Sticklers for artistic unity are well catered for by firms which make a wide variety of wallpapers and fabrics that match each other. The matching is often cunningly complementary rather than exact, scales being slightly altered, for example, or perhaps a continuous pattern from the paper appearing as the filling for additional design features on the fabric. And of course, the paper-fabric catalogues may provide an excellent source of ideas for your own combinations. If you find that the manufacturers' combinations will prove an expensive way of decorating a room, re-consider the way in which you planned to use the effect. You need not think in terms of completely covering all the walls, or hanging curtains at every available window—or indeed of using the material in such large amounts.

Why not consider a single wall papered in the relevant design, with this echoed by a table cloth, some cushions, or the seat of a chair in the matching fabric? A covered divan or a bedspread could look effective, and this in turn might be echoed by a chest-of-drawers covered with the paper, a single wall panel, a pelmet, or a set of shelves.

PLANNED AROUND TEXTURED PAPERS

Some of the types of wallpaper in the heavier-texture group are echoes of the past, having their roots in the times which knew plastering as an art rather than a trade, and in which plain, smooth surfaces held no appeal at all. Others hail from still earlier epochs, when one did not even have plaster, but lived uncomplainingly with whatever stone, wood or clay-rendering the builder chose to leave on the inside.

Wood-chip and light-embossed papers

Moulded and tooled plaster were themselves derived from intended-to-be-smooth, lime-bound roughcast, which was widely used as infill material in early timber-framed houses. Containing bulls' hair and other similar fillers to give it body, the resultant 'plaster' panels had a uniformly coarse texture which can reasonably be said to be the natural ancestor of the wood-chip papers and the shallower embossed ones now available.

Neither of these latter types is liable to demand much more in the way of hanging effort than straight, untextured paper, save perhaps a bit more patience spent in waiting for the paste to make each piece supple before it is hung. Cautionary notice: wallpapers go from unco-operatively stiff through the supple phase to end up uselessly soggy. Always watch over them and hang them as soon as they feel manageable.

Since both wood-chip and embossed papers are usually destined for a painted face, make it a clean and tidy one to start with, by hanging with as much care as if no after-treatment were planned. No light embossed paper really reacts favourably to a hard roller, even lightly used.

Trimming

Most of the wallpapers mentioned so far come to you ready-trimmed, but when you go for texture in a really ambitious way and move up into the Lincrusta league, you may perhaps find yourself faced with the job of trimming edges by hand with a heavy-duty trimming knife and a steel straight-edge. A sheet of hardboard underneath the paper will save less expendable surfaces from the inevitable scoring, and will provide an even, firm base for the process. Cut with the pattern side uppermost, unless the maker specifically recommends otherwise, and slope the knife over so that you always undercut edges. Joins finish better when you do this.

Pasting

Because it would be extremely difficult to trim after sticking down to its final resting place, you should be thankful for the stiffness of the material, which helps you to trim each piece to fit before you paste it. Heavy-duty paste is absolutely needed. As to which kind, you can safely believe either the paper or the paste maker, but do be careful to make up the paste in a way and at the strength recommended for the paper you are sticking with it: some do lesser jobs at greater dilutions.

A felt-covered roller is the tool to use for pressing Lincrusta down to the plaster, and you can use it fairly heavily. Once you have the paper anchored securely, clean off overspills of paste with a damp cloth or sponge.

Anaglyptas

When you hang Anaglyptas remember that they are essentially heavy, embossed papers. Leave appropriate paste, appropriately mixed, to soak into it until the piece is supple (but not limp). Even at the supple stage, rollers would squash the embossing you have paid for, so pay for a decent, firm-but-gentle paperhanger's brush and use it deftly to pat the piece down.

There are some Anaglyptas which come to you as high-relief panels. These are dramatic, some of them very handsome indeed, but they are moulded hollow and so appreciate special treatment. Being hollow, they will not go around internal angles. Each panel must be sponged on its back with warm water until it softens up enough for you to impose your will on it.

As it is not docile enough to allow itself to be cut in situ, you do all necessary cutting and fitting of all the panels you are going to use before you fix any of them. Accurately placed slits enable you to turn outside corners, usually convincingly. A special dextrine adhesive is buttered on to the parts that are to touch the wall, but it needs some help to take a hold, so a few panel pins will be useful here and there to tack the edges for the hour or so the dextrine takes to set.

Supaglyptas

Heaviest of all papers are the Supaglyptas, which like Lincrustas will need the services of knife and straight-edge for trimming. Suitable paste will be correspondingly thick, and it should be allowed to soak into each piece for up to a quarter of an hour. There would be little point in waiting until such heavy material went supple, but it is so thick in places that some dry patches may become visible, where the paper has drunk in all the paste originally applied. Before you put it on the wall, make sure there is a fairly even layer of adhesive showing moist on the back.

Painting

Apart from certain Lincrusta patterns which come ready-decorated, all the heavy-texture papers like emulsion paints. You may find when applying it that you will need to go to the trouble of stippling on fine-fabric effects to see that the paint does not obscure the indentations. Both stone and wood effects can be finished with proprietary scumbles, which are oily solutions with an intentionally low initial grip on the textured surface of the paper.

First, paint the paper with an oil/alkyd undercoat paint. Then, paint the scumble over about ten or twelve square ft (1-1.5m²). Use a lint-free cloth pad to wipe it off again. Wasteful though this may sound, it is not pointless, as the scumble is only wiped off the ridges, staying in the hollows to accentuate the texture. A coat of matt varnish helps to protect the finished appearance.

An alternative method to use with high-relief stone effects is to run a paint roller half-heartedly over already-dry emulsion so as to sprinkle the ridges with another colour of paint.

41 **Opposite: An anaglypta paper is here a subtle background for a well-planned room. The emphasis on texture is carried through to the bedspread and curtain, and light and shadow play important roles in creating a subtle mood of tranquillity and taste. The theme of the delicately patterned paper is reinforced by the fragility of the framed butterflies — a totally feminine room without fuss or frill.**

PAPER-BACKED FABRICS

Wallpapers have been in existence since early in the sixteenth century, so can legitimately be described as historic. But fabrics of various kinds have been hung inside human habitations for so long before that, they are all but prehistoric. Open-weave cloths made from linen or hemp fibres were used to clothe cold castle walls, and some with pictorial designs woven into them, attained the distinctive title of tapestries.

All the rough, open-weave cloths woven from natural vegetable fibres or animal wools can be thought of as a warm-wallcovering group, but there is a contrasting class of far finer cloths, silks and satins which offer overtones of oriental luxury.

Appealing as they do to our very basic instincts for warmth or for delicate tactile sensation, fabrics are often strong, first-thought favourites for lining walls. Second and third thoughts come close behind, however, and not without reason. Think carefully about management, distortion, cleaning and rot.

Most practical problems with fabrics used for decor arise from a space-restricted necessity for sticking them to walls, when their nature is to hang or drape. Their qualities of warmth and luxury are favoured, but most people fear their instability, their natural tendency to shrink or to stretch in different atmospheres, their very openness and porosity.

Helpful manufacturers are making available an ever-increasing range of fabrics conveniently mounted on paper backings, which effectively dispel all fear of movement and difficulty of hanging. The mounted materials are usually mothproofed, rot-proofed and given special treatment to make them as dirt-resistant as possible. Many of them can be cleaned by standard fabric or carpet methods, but do find out about cleaning requirements from the maker before you buy the product. Butt-joins are no more trouble to make than with wallpaper, although you have to be extremely careful not to get adhesive on the surface because of the difficulty of removing splashes completely.

Hanging fabrics
Silks and Japanese grass cloths vary both in shade and weave from one roll to another. This feature is part of their original appearance and charm, so regard it as a virtue and make the most of it by thoughtful and judicious positioning of pieces. Avoid the sharper shade gradations and start each major wall flank by hanging a complete width of paper plumb in its centre, working outwards from this key piece.

It is a waste of time to hang these fabrics directly on to the wall: lining paper, hung horizontally, is a vital prerequisite. Both silk and grass cloth paper-backed coverings have to be trimmed with a sharp knife and steel straight-edge. A $\frac{5}{8}$ in. (16mm) strip should be sliced from each side of each length before you hang it. Use old fashioned decorator's tub paste to stick it in place, but mixed to the consistency specified for the job. Soak but do not drown, and add a couple of ounces of washing soda to each bucket of paste if your fabric shows the slightest metallic colour.

Gently, gently smooth with a felt-covered roller innocent of paste, so as not to stretch or stain the delicate cloth. Adhesive must not even be allowed to squeeze from the joins. Top and bottom trimming is done extra-carefully, but normally, with super-sharp scissors. Pat into place with a paste-free hand.

Hessians and felts
Paper-backed hessians, natural or dyed, and paper-backed felts need no side-trimming as a rule, but do appreciate equally keen scissorwork at top and bottom. A special resin-filled emulsion adhesive, such as Clam 143, is the most satisfactory to use. It is usually supplied ready for use as an off-white, thick cream. Like all adhesives containing fungicides, it does not mix well with children, pets or food, so take the obvious precautions.

Put the paste on to the wall, un-diluted, but only on to one piece-area at a time, as its open-time is only generous, not unlimited. Be kind with brush or roller when you smooth pieces into place, and do not smear the surface as you trim or press.

Wool
Wool wallcoverings, although similar in principle to the other paper-backed fabrics, have their differences. They are made by fixing strands of spun wool-yarn parallel and in close touch with each other on to the paper back. Roll lengths are usually standard, but may have widths differing from those of standard wallpaper. Some patterns need trimming, others come ready-trimmed, but whether you are effecting lengthwise division for trimming or for fitting purposes, you do it by tearing, not by cutting.

Some manufacturers recommend that you lay the piece face down and hold a rule or similar straightedge firmly along your nearest strand-parting to the chosen line. Pull the first 'waste' strand gently up and backwards to produce a neat, undercut tear which will tuck out of sight behind the yarn-strand forming the new edge. Completely invisible butt-joins result. However, always check such a method first with the manufacturer.

Hanging can be done with an adhesive similar to the one used for hessian, or you can use heavy-duty vinyl-wallpaper paste. But whatever you use, paste must incorporate a fungicide, as the backing has a waterproof layer to allow the yarn to be cleaned by normal, wet carpet methods.

Standard yarn designs are both tasteful and varied, and special patterns are possible to obtain by arrangement. Those using the thicker yarns have exceptional sound-absorption qualities and are good at hiding bad walls.

Cat owners, of course, are saddled with the simple options of keeping fabric coverings six feet off the floor or resigning themselves to lengthy fringes.

42 Above: Simple luxury in an Eastern theme — with diffused light and tropical colours complementing the wall fabric. *1.* Put plenty of weight on the straightedge when trimming. Use a really sharp knife, as hessian is loosely woven and frays readily. Even a backed fabric can suffer from a blunt blade. *2.* Use a foam-sleeved roller to spread adhesive on the wall because you have to get it on evenly and quickly — very often next to an already hung length. Use it sideways near the ceiling.

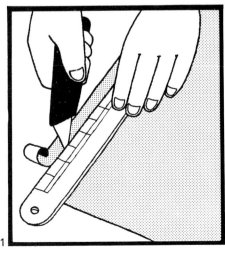

1

2

WORKING WITH NATURAL FABRICS

The first precaution to take if you are planning to decorate with unbacked fabrics is obviously to buy as little trouble with your material as possible. It is unlikely that the rolls or pieces of cloth you like were made or intended for sticking to the wall, but qualities like colour-fastness, stability under cleaning, shrink-resistance, immunity to rot and insect attack are all appreciated in applications outside the decorating field, so may quite reasonably be looked for in all but the cheapest ranges.

Fraying and shrinkage can be guarded against to a considerable extent, but lack of colour-fastness you can do very little about. Moths, however, are a fairly ubiquitous hazard, so if your fabric is not proofed against their grubs, investigate the availability of proofing solutions whose smell you can tolerate while and after applying them.

Take a really careful look at the likelihood of fraying or shrinkage giving you trouble. Fabric you are going to stick on the wall need not be cut until immediately before it is applied, so you must be pretty clumsy to achieve much shredding in the short period of risk. Major shrinkage happens when you wash cloth, or at least get it extremely wet, but wet cleaning is something you are just going to have to forget with non-purpose-made fabrics, and it would take a very damp atmosphere indeed to affect it once stuck. Attempts to pre-shrink by wetting and drying pre-cut lengths might be successful, but they can cause uneven distortion.

Adhesives
A special resin-filled emulsion adhesive, such as Clam 143, is the most practical adhesive to use for sticking coarser fabrics to the wall. Although having the consistency of thick cream, it is bound to wet the material a little, so be very stingy with the brush or foam-sleeved roller when you spread it on the wall. On non-porous walls you will have a certain freedom to slide your fabric into place, but try not to use it more than you have to, be-

cause it will be difficult not to pull the weave about in the process. If you have to mark the fabric or the wall, use pencils rather than crayons, which may bleed through it.

Splashes accidentally getting on to the fabric surface are easier to remove before they are dry, when cold water may work. Rub it on sparingly with a cloth or sponge. If the adhesive has already dried you must use Clam PVC Cleaner, a strong detergent solution, or persistent but gentle work with a suede brush.

Dealing with joins
Weave distortion can be kept to a minimum by rolling each piece around a cardboard cylinder, wooden dowel or batten, so that it can be rolled smoothly into place without multi-directional stretching. You will not be able to butt-join the sides, but overlapping will look very messy. Place the joins neatly near but leave them incomplete. They can be covered with carpet webbing, thin strips of wood or aluminium, or home-made ribbons of the fabric itself with edges folded back and stuck down with a contact adhesive such as Copydex.

Felts
Felt, of course, will pose you no problems of weave distortion, but will bring one or two of its own. It is thick heavy stuff, so has marvellous insulating properties, but it also has a goodly weight per square foot. Since rolls tend to be wider than hessian ones you may be presented with quite a load to heave up the wall. Almost certainly you will need assistance, and even with that, it could be helpful to have an extra step-ladder handy, so that you can support either end of the roll at a convenient height whilst you stick part of it down. Butt-joins are very possible, and can easily be made invisible by plucking the felt very gently with a wire brush on each side of the seam, to obscure it. Any adhesive blobs left on the surface can be removed in a similar fashion, but get them off with a damp sponge before they set, if you can.

Contact-adhesives
Strip-glueing techniques are quite feasible. Copydex (for natural cloth) or PAC (for non-absorbent materials) can be used as contact-adhesives. Coat both wall and fabric in the strips where you want them to stick. The adhesive coats should be light, and left until they are almost transparent before the fabric is put to the wall, and when it is, it must be exactly positioned. This is not easy, so you may prefer to try the same firm's double-sided adhesive tape, which you can position accurately on the wall before exposing the upper side's adhesive. Whereas this is just as instant in its grip as a smear of glue applied wet, you may find it

easier to aim for when aligning the fabric, and if you want to have folds in the fabric, you can experiment with taping those before exposing the back of the adhesive tape to the wall.

Mounting material
Uneven walls can give you more trouble than anything else when you want to use unbacked fabric for covering them. Their lumps, bumps and hollows play havoc with your joins, and can greatly mar the finished appearance of the decor. Replastering is the most radical solution, but there are feasible alternatives. If the trouble derives purely from hollows or craters, you can mount the material on frames cut from solid sheets of thin plywood, after you have painted or stained them. To get clean edges, however, the cutting would have to be done with a heavy-duty trimming knife, and patience, and a strong wrist. The technique is perhaps most useful for mounting fabric on to doors.

An alternative method is to wrap the material round sheets of thin hardboard, which can then be stuck, screwed or nailed to the wall. By nailing, you make acquaintance with masonry pins, which are hammered direct into stone or brick, without preliminary drilling or plugging. They are about as hard as your hammer-head, if not harder, and relatively brittle, so use a lot of light taps rather than a few heavy ones.

Whether you use cut-outs or hardboard to stretch your cloth over, you have the problem of attaching the edges firmly to a support some quarter of an inch thinner than the length of the shortest tack readily available. Contact adhesive is one solution, but not at all easy for the plywood-frame method. Possibly the most effective tool to use would be a small staple gun. Drawing pins would do, at a pinch.

Joins for mounted fabrics
When you use either mounting-method on walls, you will have to think of some decorative covering for the joins. Aluminium beading or thin strips of wood-moulding have the advantage over tape or webbing strips that they give the board edges some stiffening, but to do this they do need to be firmly nailed through to the wall behind.

Remember that some mouldings may be thin enough to split when even quite small pins are tapped through them. To avoid the danger, drill small holes for the pins, only slightly smaller in diameter than the pins themselves, and tap all the pins into the beading before you offer it up to the wall. Use a punch for the last fraction of an inch.

43 Right: Coloured felt is ideal to use when a cosy atmosphere is wanted. If neat seams are a problem, cover them with carpet webbing, as seen here.

1. The broader your 'rolling pin' the better when hanging unbacked fabrics. Remember the batten at the bottom is to be removed, so make sure it comes well below your trimming line. *2.* You can choose from a wide variety of materials to cover up the inevitably untidy butt joins between adjacent lengths of fabric.

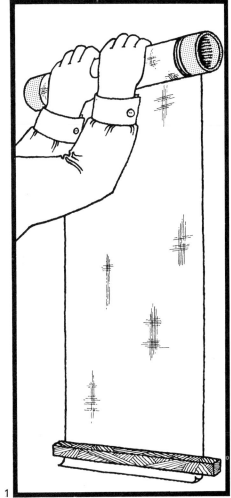

1

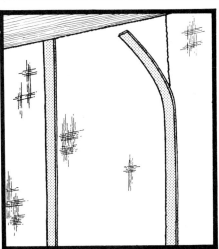

2

44 Left: Clever use of paper and fabric here combine to disguise pipes and an awkwardly positioned closet.

45 Below: To relieve the totality of the pattern, a softly coloured spread; some cushions; flowers to echo these.

USING PAPERS TO DISGUISE PROBLEMS

1. There is no chance at all of matching the pattern when you bandage pipes like this, but the technique does soften the glaring functionalism of naked metal. Do not try to work with too long a strip at a time: this is neither possible nor needful. All joins between strip ends go at the back. Make no attempt to paper the valve. **2.** Large diameter pipes can accommodate much more generous units of camouflage. Unless they are in the room centre, you can overlap the joins out of sight. Even with undisguised joints this pipe's enormity no longer obtrudes.

1

2

A continuous pattern in wallpaper can be a tremendous advantage in helping to disguise those uninvited bulges and unwished-for protrusions that elbow their presence into our living-quarters. Regardless of when a house was built, there always seems to be some service or structural member that no one thought to make provision for until the main walls, ceilings and floors were all solidly in position. Faced at this late stage with the necessity of hiding away some pipe, duct, cable, or even roof-beam or staircase which cuts diagonally through the last remaining clear space, the builder has quickly put together a scratch casing of boards and plaster to put the eyesore conveniently out of sight. But not so conveniently out of mind.

Camouflaging

The essential nature of these obstructive pillars and boxes makes it almost impossible to get rid of them, even with the most ingenious home surgery. Few of them are worthy of being made into features, so you have to resort to the wiles of camouflage.

Think for a moment about the nature of camouflage, about the purpose of it, and about the principles successfully used by the military practitioners. You will not often see a camouflaged gun or vehicle painted with a small-motif pattern, or with any colours which are liable to make it stand out from its surroundings. The whole object of the weirdly amorphous stripes and patches is to break up the clear outline of the camouflaged item, to lead the eye over the sharp edges, across the vital, identifying contours to the terrain adjoining, so that the shape for which the enemy eyes are searching appears to merge with what is around it. You know the gun is there but at least its presence is more of a whisper than a bellow, which is the best *you* can hope to achieve.

Using patterns

While all patterned papers will make some improvement, perhaps the least effective are plain patterns, uniformly textured ones, regular-spots, formalized flowers or leaves in marshalled rows, tiles, wooden board effects and pictorial designs. If your nuisance is a simple and regular step, level and with angles which are more or less right, the larger, bold and vertical patterns will not be too difficult to manoeuvre into the angles. More irregular geometry could, however, give you pattern-continuity problems, and that the pattern should carry on uninterrupted around the ridges is vital to success.

After all, it cannot be an accident that the traditional treatment for the shelving slopes and tight turnings of attic rooms has become herbs and flowerets growing gloriously upwards and burgeoning around the banisters.

Few other types of patterns have quite the flair as these for choking obstructions into insignificance. If the cutting and fitting you have to do does happen to break a few stems, there are many others for the eye to pick up nearby.

Outstanding ridges

Vertical ridges projecting from a wall are ideal subjects for papers having strong horizontal features, which can most effectively reduce the prominence of adjoining pillars. As in all disguising operations, you should so organize the joins that they do not have to be made on the face of the problematic form. The feeling that the pattern continues right around without noticing the interruption must be preserved.

Pipes

Exposed pipes pose all the problems of boxes and beams, together with one or two of their own. The ones left out in the open are usually those which did not run sufficiently close to angles for easy boxing in, or close enough to walls for hiding under plaster. Some form of camouflage is practically the only expedient you can adopt. Narrow diameter pipes are less obtrusive to start with, although much trickier than water-main bores to stick paper to.

Priming metal pipes

Most small pipes are metal, which unless it is painted is not liked by many wallpaper adhesive solutions. You may, then, have to use a priming paint to be certain of unspoilt results.

Perfect blending with the papered surface behind just is not possible because of differences in parallax bound to occur as you move about the room, so match any paper on it to look about right from the door. Thinner diameters may have to be spirally bandaged with narrow strips of paper, but if you can fold wider pieces around, to join invisibly at the back, the matching will be better.

Other problems

Fittings, such as nuts and valves, which bulge out unsmoothly are best left unpapered, unless it is possible to make a neat job of them. The same goes for the swollen joints of the larger monumental cylinders. If you cannot cover these completely, you can at least reduce their impact by using the larger-scale designs on those portions which are possible to cover.

STICK ON A DESIGN

Selective use of any thin sheet material is feasible, whether or not its maker intended it to be stuck on ceilings and walls. This means looking at papers, fabrics, metallic foils and plastic-faced decorating materials in a light entirely different from the accepted one of regarding them as total coverage for complete sections. Instead, look at stick-on sheet decor as judiciously placed highlight potential for lending a little life and interest to plainer or less colourful grounds.

Motif designs in foil

Very many wallpaper designs contain features which you can extract bodily by cutting precisely around their outlines, so that they can be transferred to prepared backgrounds on which they become dramatic and graceful features. Backed metallic sheeting or unbacked foil can be cut into shapes like stars or crescent moons. Most can be stuck successfully with standard vinyl adhesives, which all incorporate the fungicides necessary when waterproof coverings are put down.

You may have to think more in terms of foil somewhat thicker than that sold for cookery. The same manufacturers can normally supply it, or will indicate another source if you draw a blank expression in the shops. Foils pasted on to broader surfaces, especially if they have been cut into complex forms first, can be difficult to clean. If you do fear discolouration, lacquer them as soon as they are stuck firm.

Remember that metallic surfaces often appreciate a reassuringly alkaline one underneath, which washing soda in the paste can provide for them.

It's in the field of itsy-bitsy decorative touches or of high-impact treatment of significant limited areas that self-adhesive coverings come into their own. Put out of your mind any half-remembered horrors of the past and base your judgment of where to use them on the very much altered modern products—as far removed from oilcloth imitating gingham as you can imagine.

Fablon

Change the old and enhance the new has always been the message by which self-adhesive magic has been sold. Justifiably at that, especially in its modern forms. There are now as many as five different effects you can choose from in self-adhesive, plastic-finished coverings (e.g. Fablon), in no less than 28 patterns, all modern in style.

Four of them are made from PVC, just as vinyl wallpapers are, their surfaces being correspondingly tough and scrubbable. The great advantage of self-stick material, however, is its instant quality. Finished the second you press the final corner down, it offers great reward for little labour.

Its adhesive is extremely strong, and has high initial tack, so it pays to get it in the right position on the first try. If you do manage to make a crease or a bubble by virtue of determined inattention, you can peel the sheet partly back and put things right, but not too many times.

Cut it precisely to the shape you want before peeling off the backing, and make sure that the surface is free from grease and loose dirt before you do that. Not that these materials will not stick gamely enough to unscoured under-surfaces, but you cannot expect them to stay down long. All self-adhesives work best on a really clean, non-greasy base. The nearer you get to pre-paint astringency, the better the adhesive will perform, particularly with regard to edge-grip, which is what longevity depends on. Absorbent surfaces also work against successful sticking. New or any other unpainted wood or plaster should be sealed before you start.

Perhaps the most widely used form of self-adhesive covering is the continuous roll, which you can buy as long as you are likely to want, and up to a yard (1m) wide. If you put this on tabletops or drawer fronts, avoid finishing on corners. Take it around if you can to a place where it can anchor its edge on the flat.

Smooth, clear glass can be quickly textured with a special translucent version (e.g. Decroglaze). When using this material, it might be better to edge

trim after pressing it into the angle between glass and frame, rather as you trim wallpaper.

Continuous panoramic mural strips, and friezes for children's rooms complete the PVC surfaced armoury, but one supremely useful product remains in the self-adhesive group. It consists of nylon, flocked on to a self-stick base to give a bright, soft, felt appearance to what is a hard-wearing and resilient velour. It can line drawers, back bookshelves, pad lamp or vase bottoms, or just look rich in full view.

46 Right: It's so easy to make your own patterns for wall decorations. Self-adhesive papers are quite readily available, and mean that all you need do is cut out shapes and stick them on. The silver design used here adds a contrasting texture and dimension to the deep blue of the walls.

1. Use a simple template for the shape you want — a saucer would be ideal. Draw around it with a soft pencil, on the backed side of the foil, and cut accurately around the pencil line with really sharp scissors. If you plan to use semi-circles, cut them now.
2. After cutting as many shapes as you need for your design, carefully prise up the edge of the foil and pull it slowly away from the backing material. It is a good idea to pause halfway across, to allow static electricity to disperse.
3. Position the foil against the wall on a pre-drawn chalk line (use the original template to mark out a design, if you like). Make sure the foil is level and correctly positioned. As long as you do not stick it down completely, you should be able to lift the disc and move it once or twice. Finally, rub it down firmly with a soft cloth, to disperse any air bubbles.

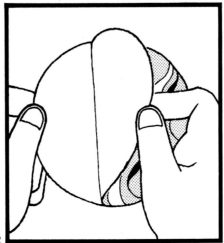

47 Above: Here, a wallpaper border made from a cut-out strip of a large repeating pattern has been used in the archway to bridge the entrance from one room to another.

48 Right: Wallpaper borders can be used as contrasts too. Take them along skirting boards and up corners, as in this child's playroom. Or use them to create small panelled areas in a painted room. As long as you pay attention to colour scheming, you can use such borders almost anywhere.

CONTRAST OR COMPLEMENT WITH WALLPAPER BORDERS

When wallpaper covers the whole of a wall, and you have trimmed it accurately to merge straight into whatever surface adjoins, you have made a background, which is in all probability appreciated only in passing. Perhaps your intention stops there, but sometimes you may desire a more positive effect, want people to pay your wall a degree of attention more like that which they would accord a framed picture.

Bordering wallpaper with contrasting or complementary patterned additional papers is by no means a new device, but a well-tried and time-honoured one, creeping back into favour under a number of contemporary stimuli. Not the least of these is the disappearance from modern houses of picture rails and generous skirting-boards. Although these features might, especially if put in as afterthoughts, look incongruously out of proportion to the scale of new interiors, interfering grotesquely with their clean, sheer planes.

All the same, the feeling that you should do something to break up today's floor-to-ceiling flanks to give them definition and character is understandable. They are completely blank canvases, at one and the same time limitless opportunities for decoration and bewildering challenges for the decorator. Using wallpaper borders is just one way of making the most of them.

Strip borders

A border gives a wall a certain dominance, making you look, as it does, with added intensity at the paper it encloses. One word of advice is never to detract from this effect by topping the border with a frieze. (A door-top to cornice frieze, that is. You can call a border a frieze quite legitimately, and some manufacturers sell them as such, but we have maintained the distinction for clarity.)

Most wallpaper firms put out ranges of paired patterns, one bold-feature and a smaller and plainer companion to complement it. One of the simplest bordering expedients you can try is to cut strips from the subservient pattern to frame the dominant one, running your border all around the edges of each wall flank. Only rarely is the main pattern suitable for reversing the roles. This will entail mitring corners after exact measurement, but you will have this to do even if you use one of the border strips made by some firms, especially for the job. A small, plastic setsquare is adequate for marking the necessary 45° angles, but not for using as a knife guide. Mark with a pencil and cut to your line.

Framing

Golden rules could easily be made up to tell you how wide to make your borders, but the only reliable guide is in your own eye. If you cannot sense the width at which your border becomes a blind, you probably will not be attracted to the idea of using a framing technique in the first place. The human eye has shrewd judgment, so trust it.

Borders can, of course, frame off selected wall sections instead of defining the periphery, or make frames in addition to that. This is a very effective method of combating the raincloud 'loomingness' of large wall flanks, or of giving form and orientation to a featureless room. Pictures or other hung items can find a valuably stabilized environment within a well-proportioned frame.

Panels

To give even more eminence to a handsome wallpaper, you can mount a large panel of it at the visual centre of a wall, so that the space between the border around the panel and the wall's boundary is left plainly painted, devoid of pattern. One development of this technique of frame-emphasis is the abandonment of borders *of* wallpaper and the substitution of non-paper borders *for* wallpaper. These can be made from a variety of materials limited only by your imagination—one of the most obviously suitable being wood, natural, stained, painted, polished, or even ebonized.

Wooden frames are fairly simple to put up, and need be no more permanent than the paper, since they carry no more load than their own weight. Carpet webbing borders can be used, dyed if you like, as can aluminium strip, petersham ribbon, your pick of other fabrics, or soft plastic edging which is sold mainly for shelves and tables. Most of these materials can be fixed to a wall with contact adhesives.

Variations

Because of the impermanence and adaptability of the bordering materials, further experimentation is only a step along the road, fraught with neither danger nor unpleasantness. From one large frame you may graduate to several smaller ones which you can set up and site so as to make the best possible improvement to the shape of the room, giving it an air of originality at the same time. Nor need the panels be oblong. With a sense of proportion and a little ingenuity, you can ring the changes almost indefinitely.

USE FLOOR TILES FOR WALLS TOO

Essentially a carpet is a background to gracious living—smooth, warm and soft. Eastern in origin, it began as a wall-hanging and has retained throughout its long history a persistent adaptable personality.

From its role as a tapestry, it first descended to the floor in the capacity of table-cloth. Hence the phrase 'on the carpet' came into being. Originally it meant on the agenda because parleys and conferences used to be held around a rug on the ground, long before tables and chairs took over.

Wool has never really fallen from favour as a carpeting material; even the man-made fibres which are now mixed with it and substituted for it have to imitate its essential characteristics of warmth and resilience in order to be popular. Since the desire to seek warmth is very high in the order of priority among basic human drives, this state of affairs is unlikely to change in the forseeable future.

Following the introduction of wool yarns for wall decoration, carpets now are beginning to regain their appeal as woven pictures. While it would be ludicrous to reflect this trend by tacking a yard or two of broadloom to the wall, it might be reasonably argued that an attractive rug could offer as great and positive a feeling of comfort hung prominently as it would spread underfoot. In the latter instance its appeal is at least as much tactual as it is visual, and in all probability more so.

Types of carpet
Discounting coloured felts, sisal or coco-fibre mattings, which (whatever their virtues) are of a somewhat different nature, there are for practical purposes two main groups of carpets: those with a rubber backing and those without.

True carpets are made by hooking tufts of wool-fibre, or modern substitutes for it, into a simply-woven jute fabric resembling sacking. This backing is selvedged at the sides of the rolls of carpet as they are made, but when it is cut, there is nothing to stop the jute strands from unravelling and the tufts from becoming unanchored.

Rubber coating applied to the backing effectively prevents this fraying, but also stops cleaning solutions from passing through; perhaps an advantage when you clean carpets in situ, but presenting difficulty to professional cleaners, who dry the unbacked type more easily.

Obviously, even unbacked carpets must be cut, and kept from disintegrating in the process. The traditional method, still widely employed by professionals, is to bind the backing by stitching. However, you can now get rubber-latex based binding adhesives which allow you to do a very effective edge or join without special skill. These glues are usually used in combination with broad strips of binding tape, which are tapped on to the backing with a hammer.

Although this method makes a very firm and neat join, some of the adhesives on the market are broken up by dry-cleaning chemicals, so if you intend to send your carpet to be professionally cleaned eventually, have it stitched.

Trimming to fit
Trimming knives with heavy-duty blades are normally the tools for cutting carpets, but there are more sophisticated cutters about, with guiding plates and flat-iron handle-grips. If you want to fit an all-over patterned or plain carpet into a defined area, you will find it easier to lay the bulk, joining as necessary, to within a foot or so of the edge to which you are working. Then take a separate piece and cut one edge to fit your skirting or other boundary. The join with the main carpet can be made by cutting through both layers as they lie overlapped, removing the waste scraps and taping the now invisible joint.

Vinyl tiles
This technique can also serve very well for fitting sheet vinyls, but these are far simpler to handle in the form of tiles. Always start by finding the true middle of the area you want to cover, discounting bays and alcoves, and drawing diagonals between opposing corners of the main field. From the point where they intersect, draw lines to the centre points of the shorter pair of opposing walls. These and the diagonally derived centre point will enable you to lay four tiles from which all the others can be aligned.

Most suitable adhesives take the form of pastes, which you spread evenly with a special comb. 'Butter' a square yard (about 1m) at a time, pressing the tiles into position straightaway.

When you have worked to within one tile-width of all edges, mark and cut boundary tiles individually to fit the remaining spaces. For more-or-less square spaces (in fact, all those without odd contours or mitred angles)

you can chalk the edges of the tiles already laid, turn each tile to be fitted on to its back with its edge pressed up to the wall, and snap its free side on to the chalked edge. Cut off the waste, turn the cut tile the right way around and it will fit accurately.

For odd shapes and contours you will need to make an accurate template of the shape and trace it on to the tile. Special comb-like proprietary tools are available which are a great help in tracing out almost *any* shape.

Carpet-tiling walls
Carpet tiles, the latest development of the carpet theme, make a rich, warm alternative to other coverings for the occasional wall. They are well-adapted for the job and offer useful sound and heat insulation. Since they interlock, the first row needs to be mounted as horizontally as you can make it.

Most makes have an impervious backing, such as polypropylene, so the surface they are stuck to must be dry, and the adhesive used must be chosen with care. Preferably, it should incorporate a fungicide. It should not contain latex or any organic compound, it should set hard and have strong initial tack. See which of those advised by the tile maker best suits your wall.

If the tiles are used only part way up a wall, wooden beading or metal carpet-finishing trim can be used to neaten the top edge.

49 Opposite: Make a drab seating area look like new—two panels of floor tiles used on the walls, some carefully chosen accessories, a touch of paint, and it's a whole new atmosphere. Try using tiles to repeat the floor theme in an alcove too.

1. It is far easier to fit narrow widths into irregular edges than broad ones. For complex mouldings, jigs like this shape-tracer can be a great help. Always start edge-fitting using the farthest boundary as your guide. In this case, it would be the line

where the next carpet starts.
2. Having completed the edge contours, fit the boundary strip of carpet into place, then overlap the main body with its unshaped edge. With the guidance of a straight-edge, cut through both layers of carpet. This leaves you two

waste strips.
3. When the waste strips are removed, the fitted pieces of carpet should meet exactly. It is better for the underlay to be joined elsewhere if possible.
4. The two mating edges can be joined by a single broad strip of

carpet tape. This will also have a sealing effect if your carpet is not rubber backed, but in that case you might be well advised to seal with additional tape or a stronger solution, before joining the edges together.

WAYS WITH COLOUR SCHEMES

50 Each of the four columns below shows possible colour combinations which may be applied to decorating schemes ; the pentagon, top right, gives a selection of neutrals which may be used with any colour choices.

From left to right: **1.** Shades of single colours, with their possible accenting colours. **2.** Three-colour combinations and their accents or contrasts. **3.** Two-colour contrasts with their possible accents. **4.** Multi-colour combinations to experiment with.

Use these schemes only as a guide. Colour balance — more of one, less of another — is always necessary, but our proportions need not be followed. And remember colour balance does not apply only to walls and woodwork — all furnishings should also play a part.

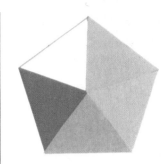

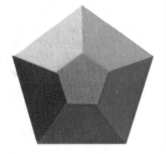
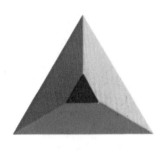

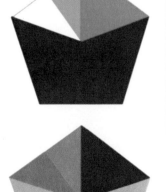

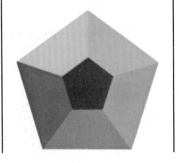

SECOND-HAND BARGAINS MADE NEW

Finding unusual furniture for the home is fun – and especially rewarding if you come across a bargain. Often the most original or inspiring interiors are those which have been carefully put together from a range of assorted furniture styles and finishes – richly grained polished woods and veneers of almost any period, painted or stained chairs and tables of a more modern, mass-produced variety, or huge, old cupboards and chests brought to life with linings of pretty paper.

Variety of finishes

Whatever your tastes, most second-hand furniture can be refinished to suit you. Whether you want to strip wood to enhance the grain, give it a shiny polish, stain it a brilliant colour, paint it with a gloss finish or decorate it with unusual designs, it's quite easy to do if you follow a few basic rules when you first examine your chosen piece. You can even give wood a ready-made antique finish using a proprietary preparation.

What to avoid

Never attempt to renovate anything which might be valuable or classed as an antique – if in doubt consult an expert before doing any work.

Look at all structural repairs, such as broken chair or table legs, damaged upholstery or badly chipped wood, in relation to your own practical skills. Simple repairs for beginners are given in this book, but if you have to pay a skilled craftsman to repair a piece for you, you will no longer have a bargain.

Finally, examine all wood for traces of woodworm – it's death to furniture and can easily infect any wooden structures. It can be identified by fine round holes and powdery wood dust. Very mild cases can be treated with proprietary anti-woodworm solutions, but advanced cases are difficult to cure, so avoid them.

Other 'junk' items

Apart from wooden furniture, other useful or decorative bits and pieces will benefit from some renovation. Silver, glass, china – and things made from copper, brass, chrome or marble – can be given new life with a bit of careful work, so don't pass them by.

Remember: with careful examination and preparation, you can make a secondhand bargain into an attractive addition to any home.

WHAT TO LOOK FOR

Most of the old furniture you will come across will be made almost entirely of wood, which was available to craftsmen of earlier times in copious quantities and great variety. To make the best possible assessment of secondhand pieces, the more you know about wood the better.

Grain markings
In temperate conditions trees make new tissue at a very high rate in the spring, but slower in the summer, and concentric rings of wood are added as it grows fatter. Spring growth is lighter coloured and somewhat softer than the narrower bands of summer wood — which form 'annual rings', most marked in softwoods.

How logs are cut up
It is the tree's annual rings of summer tissue that form the characteristic grain stripes of the wood when the trunk is sawn lengthwise into boards and battens.

By no means all the log is usable wood, so the timber merchant's main concern is to get as much saleable material as he can. He normally slices softwoods into slabs, with parallel sawcuts which give him a good chance of wasting little but the bark and the central pith of a sound log. Although this method yields perfectly adequate timber for common building purposes, it is far from satisfactory for furniture. Every plank, except those on either side of the pith, tends to curl up away from the centre as it dries out and ages. The middle two planks have equal stresses on both broad surfaces so their movement is minimal.

Quarter-sawn virtues
Looking at these centre-slice boards end-on, you will see that the ring markings are almost at right angles to their faces. This feature is what you should look for to check whether your wood is radially sawn. Some boards will be cut perfectly 'on the quarter' ('quarter sawn' and 'radially sawn' are often used interchangeably). This method means that only four pieces can be removed from a log, so various patterns of log conversion have been evolved to give customers fairly stable stock at reasonable prices. Quarter sawing is inevitably more expensive than plain sawing because it wastes a good part of the log.

Grain figure
Some hardwoods are sawn radially for another reason. They have very visible rays — thin curtains of storage cells which are hung in straight lines radiating from the centre of the tree to its perimeter. Softwoods have them as well but they are not visible and the hardwood ones only show themselves to full advantage in fully quarter-sawn planks. For this reason you may see timber in some merchants' catalogues that is advertised as 'quarter sawn but not necessarily fully figured'. Not that there aren't other kinds of grain figure, resulting perhaps, from twisting growth or knots but rays in hardwoods are the main source where solid wood is concerned.

Veneers
Exotic, richly hued and beautifully figured timbers have always been in shorter supply than run-of-the-mill varieties. As well as being scarcer, the knotted or twisted kinds are by and large too weak structurally to be of much use in normal joinery. Knowing this, many successive generations of carpenters have used such wood in thin sheets to veneer plainer but stronger materials. Rarer veneers became expensive, and naturally fell into the hands of only the most skilful craftsmen. They developed the art of matching veneers: taking adjacent sheets from the same log, which of course had the same figuring, and arranging them in symmetrical patterns to cover broad surfaces.

Know your timbers
As species and sub-species run literally into the thousands, you would need to be an expert indeed to name different woods on sight. However, in the secondhand furniture field, you have a relatively small selection to familiarize yourself with. If starting from scratch, buy a set of educational samples from a merchant and study the grains, which are a surer guide than colour (often disguised by varnish). Look at a lot of museum pieces. This will give you a fair idea of which kinds of wood are used to make different sorts of pieces. Always try to see through the finish to the wood, so that you don't scrape off or paint over anything worth salvaging.

Know your finishes
There are few surface finishes on furniture which are incapable of being restored, so don't bypass a charming piece just because its surface is in bad condition.

Some finishes cover up the wood underneath or disguise it, while others enhance the wood without covering the grain. Below is a quick guide to the basic types of finishes and where you might expect to find them:

Oiled finishes will darken the wood but allow the grain and texture to show through. Oak, deal and beech furniture was traditionally finished with oil and wax, or with oil and a turpentine-gum based varnish. The latter is not used today.

Wax polishes were traditionally made from a mixture of beeswax, turpentine and carnauba wax. Modern wax finishes are made with silicone ingredients and are more resistant to marking. This type of polish is used mainly to protect another finish, such as oil.

Varnishes come in numerous varieties and combinations. Some are based on natural wood resins, others on synthetic cellulose constituents, and still others are based on shellac and a volatile spirit mixture.

Older types of furniture were often covered with varnishes known as lacquers, which were usually spirit varnishes. Most mass-produced furniture made within the last 40 years (except reproduction furniture and that with a polyurethane finish) was covered with a cellulose-based lacquer. This can be identified by the thick, layered appearance of the surface coating.

French polish is a traditional finish often found on antique furniture. It is composed chiefly of shellac dissolved in methylated spirits, but the mirror-like surface which is characteristic of this polish is achieved through the actual polishing technique.

Painted finishes are, of course, easily recognized. If you find a fairly old painted piece, do not be too hasty about removing the paint. Some old paints can in themselves make a piece of furniture valuable. If in doubt, seek a professional appraisal.

Caveat emptor
(Let the buyer beware)
Never mind the dirt or the broken legs, but avoid loose joints in any quantity, panels with broad cracks in them or tide-marked wood betraying exposure to damp. Above all, keep a sharp lookout for signs of attack by fungi and wood-boring pests. Train your nose to differentiate between the dusty and the musty. Shun pieces with clumsy repairs that destroy the original character of the piece: screws visibly placed, nailed patches, metal rods or wires. Most broken legs can be repaired, the simpler ones possibly replaced. But if you come across an elaborately curved one with a compound fracture involving splits down the grain and loss of timber, remember that you won't be able to mend or to replace it yourself unless you have skills equivalent to those of the original maker.

51 The table: You may find a deep dovetail joint (inset left) where apron and side join the leg top. If you do not want to replace the joint with hand-made dovetails, use dowels.
The top is usually held down by turn buttons (inset right). These are not glued, since they have to be free to slide a little in their grooves as the top wood shrinks with time.
The chest with sagging drawers: There are often small plywood anti-wear pads, pinned and glued to the drawer rails. If you replace them, lay the new pieces with the top grain running from back to front, otherwise the sliding action of the drawer may splinter them. Use a diamond with a point facing front (inset right).
The drawer-separating rails are probably fitted into the sides with stub tenons (inset left) so are not easily replaced. You must cut out worn corners and fit matching inserts.
The chest's top is fixed on to struts joined to the frame with small dovetails.

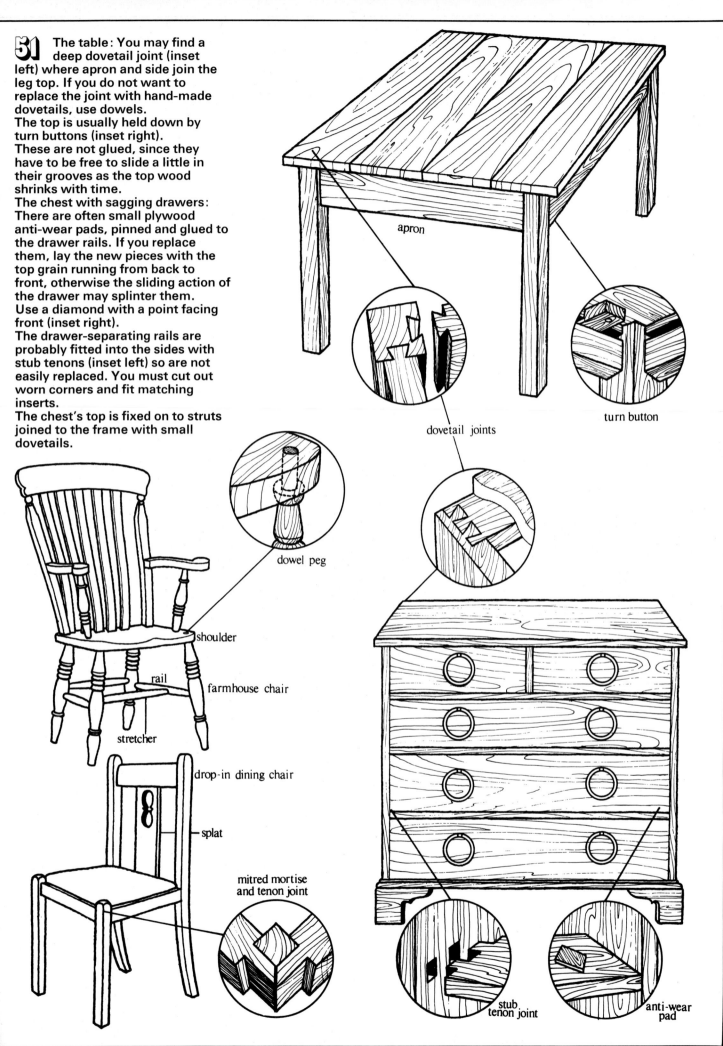

apron

turn button

dovetail joints

dowel peg

shoulder

rail

farmhouse chair

stretcher

drop-in dining chair

splat

mitred mortise and tenon joint

stub tenon joint

anti-wear pad

BASIC CLEANING AND RENOVATING

In the cold light of home, you will probably be able to make a more detailed and objective assessment of the state of your find than was possible when you first examined it. Remember, if it looks a fine, well-made piece of furniture, have it appraised by an expert before you do any work on it — some pieces are worth more in their original (possibly damaged) state than they would be after any but expert restoration.

Identifying the polish
Patina, the deep surface finish that is built up by the years and loving care, cannot be instantly recreated, so never remove it unless it is absolutely unavoidable. Be especially careful with oiled and waxed finishes on stained or natural wood. Applied finishes such as varnish, French polish or paint can be touched up in local spots if necessary. However modern finishes differ considerably in composition from old ones and it may be difficult, without experience, to achieve a good match with materials that will adhere to and blend in with the old surface. A bit of careful experimentation on scraps of wood or unseen areas of the furniture can prove invaluable.

To distinguish one finish from another rub real turpentine (not a mineral substitute) onto a small area with a soft cloth, where the spot will not show. If the wood has been oiled and waxed, a rub or two with the turpentine will take you down to the bare wood. If a polished surface is still visible after the turps test, rub on a little methylated spirit. The surface will go sticky and soft if it has been French polished.

Yet another test for ascertaining a finish is to scrape a small, unnoticeable area with a razor blade. French polish should produce very thin shavings or curls; oil varnishes produce thicker shavings; and cellulose varnishes will only scrape to powder.

If you decide to refinish completely, you will of course have to start by stripping off the old top-dressing. This is a major operation, dealt with more fully on pages 74 and 75. But what about simple cleaning and retouching?

Beware of the bathtub
Whatever you do, don't pour gallons of soapy water over it and scrub it clean. Dirt may respond to this treatment, but the wood may not like it at all. Two major problems are likely to occur from such treatment: the wood will either become flexible and warp, or its moisture content will rise above 20 per cent so that it begins to rot. Either way, the dampness will make the grain rise, because spring wood absorbs water more quickly than summer growth. This is how the ridges occur on scrubbed deal table tops. Hardwoods react far less violently, certain types having tremendous natural resistance to penetration. Chestnut, oak and teak are the ones you are likely to come across, but pieces made from these should still not be scrubbed or doused, for fear of water affecting the animal glue which holds the joints together.

Solvents and scrape
If your piece is relatively lightly soiled, a well-squeezed washleather and mild detergent may be enough to clean it. Nothing more astringent should be tried on French polish, but paints, varnishes or lacquers could be cleaned with any proprietary paint cleaner. After washing and thoroughly drying the wood you can decide whether the surface needs nothing more than a good waxing, or whether any scratches, dents or burns need repairing or retouching before the piece can be used. (See pages 72, 73, 74, 75.)

Removing old wax
Before any repair can be made which involves applying fresh French polish all trace of wax polish and sticky oil must be removed. Where you intend confining your repairs to a local patching job, subsequently merging new polish into the old, use cotton wool soaked in a mineral turpentine substitute to mop the surface and dissolve the wax, followed by a good scrub with a clean, absorbent rag. Knitting needles or suitably whittled hardwood sticks are useful for getting into the moulding crannies.

As it is now so easy to apply a proprietary French polish on top of the old, you may decide to repolish the piece completely. If so, you could use very fine steel wool instead of cotton wool to clean the surface. Small areas of damaged French polish can be removed in the same manner using a proprietary varnish remover, or very strong ammonia.

Paints and varnishes
You can treat small areas of paint, varnish or lacquer in a similar way, with an appropriate solvent.

Test for the best solvent to use on a small, unnoticeable area; methylated spirit, acetone, cellulose thinners or proprietary strippers are some common solvents. Always exercise extreme caution when working with them; keep away from fire and be sure to work where there is good ventilation.

Remove the damaged area only, unless the whole surface has crazed into tiny cracks, or has badly bloomed to a milk-white opacity.

Veneers versus solids
Many pieces of old or secondhand furniture are entirely surfaced with sheets of polished veneer. A careful look at the end grain along the vertical edge of a flat surface will usually reveal enough of a difference in the grains for you to determine whether or not the piece is veneered. Repairs to veneered surfaces are discussed on pages 72, 73, but it is possible to deal with superficial scratches or marks as you would with solid wood.

It is essential to remember that a veneer is very thin and has been fixed on its base with Scotch glue, so great care must be taken not to let water or other solvents soak into the bare wood. If the water gets under the veneer, it will lift and you will have a very major restoration job to do. Veneers or marquetry inlays were never varnished with anything containing turpentine or its substitutes, as these would also have softened the glue. Quick drying volatile spirit varnishes were used instead.

Further considerations
Always think of the wood which lies beneath the surface finish and then decide what type of finish would best suit the appearance of the wood and the use to which you are going to put the piece. *Oiled finishes* darken wood without covering the grain or texture. The finish is quite tough, water resistant, and non-gloss. In general, softwoods are not suitable for oiling. *Wax polishes* are excellent protectors for oiled or French-polished surfaces. If applied to raw wood, the wood should first be sealed with a modern polyurethane sealer.

Varnishes will give wood a transparent, hard-gloss finish. As has been mentioned, there are many different types of varnish which have been used at different times on furniture. Modern synthetic surface finishes, composed of polyurethanes, give the same effect as varnishes. These are easy to apply and are more resistant to heat, water, scratches or spirits than either cellulose lacquers or French polish (the latter, especially, is very easily marked by liquids or heat).

If you do discover that your piece needs some structural repairs, tackle these before you touch up the finish — a variety of common repairs are described on pages 72 and 73.

52 Left: Many pieces of furniture only need a good clean and polish before they are fit for use. A dirty, greasy surface can generally be cleaned with a soft cloth and a solution of warm water and mild detergent – a pure white soap is very good.

Always wring out the cloth so that it is damp, not wet. Light wood, such as was used for the Welsh dresser, is often covered with sticky polish or even varnish or lacquer. Once you have removed the finish, you may find the natural grain only needs a good wax for protection.

Below: When cleaning a wood surface, be sure you do not take off the deep mellow patina by using very abrasive tools. Old wax can be removed by a very light rub with scouring powder and a dry cloth (never use water), and an appropriate grade of steel wool is best for crevices and turnings.

TOOLS AND HOW TO USE THEM

When renovating secondhand furniture the correct use of a few basic tools will make all the difference between a haphazard and a professional-looking job.

Personal protection equipment

An enormous amount of the work involved in renovating things consists of hard, dirty tasks, involving exposure to dust, chemicals and assorted nuisances of various kinds. Think ahead and protect yourself adequately. It is really only common sense to use breathing masks, safety goggles, barrier creams or gloves. Suit them to the job: for example, use plastic gloves instead of rubber ones when you have oils, greases or petroleum-derived solvents to deal with. Any of these will quickly make rubber gloves swell to twice their original size and finally disintegrate.

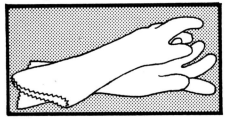

Cabinet and makeshift scrapers

To a carpenter, a scraper means considerably more than a sharp edge dragged at right angles across a wood surface. What he uses is a razor-keen, smoothly honed steel blade with the cutting edge burred over at a fairly acute angle to form a minute hook which slices off incredibly fine shavings from the timber. The finish which is left on the wood is so smooth that only a rub with the finest abrasive paper is needed to finish off. Today, it would probably be a very experienced craftsman who had mastered the techniques of sharpening and using the traditional hand scraper, and he would almost certainly have made it himself from a piece of silver (saw) steel.

Hand blades are still made by smaller tool firms, but the market leaders have concentrated on a two-handled model looking rather like an outsize metal spokeshave — far easier to sharpen and to use. Bevelled at 45°, its blade is honed exactly like a chisel, then the edge is turned over. Burnishers being scarce, smooth screwdriver blades are used instead. The set on this kind of scraper is produced by a small screw, mounted in the centre, which bends the edge downwards when it is turned.

Blades for these handled models have one curved edge for stripping off old paints and polishes quickly and one straight edge for finishing work. Their main drawback is that they are only meant to be used on flat or convex surfaces.

When you need a scraper to get into an angle or a rebate, the best solution is to turn over the edge of a chisel. Do not expect long life from a chisel converted to such a use and do not expect to use it for cabinet work ever again. All the same, you still need to use a good, plastic-handled type, to resist the pull of the scraping action.

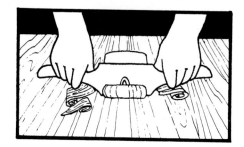

Holding devices

For some reason not easily explained, tools and equipment in this category seem to be the last that many people consider buying, whereas they are nearly the most important of all. No matter how many tools you may have, you will always have difficulty in working effectively unless you can hold things down firmly.

This does not necessarily mean that you must have a work bench, although there are some very compact, folding kinds now available. Portable vices mounted on trestles or tables, or even on stepladders, are a great help. (Always prop stepladders firmly open first.) Some self-grip wrenches have special clamps available as accessories, which enable them to be used as miniature vices. Multi-purpose vices offer tremendous versatility and value for money. They are probably the best type to get if you have no storage space and must manage all your repairs on the kitchen table.

Weights are another useful device to have. They make effective stabilizing influences on horizontal boards and can help a lot with gluing jobs – the only possible difficulty being that you must leave them in position until the setting is completely finished.

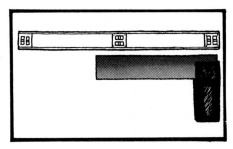

Reference tools

Straightedges are quite expensive, and easily worn untrue by constant duty as knife guides. Secondhand steel rules in the region of a metre long are reasonably priced and perfectly adequate for most of the jobs you are likely to do. If you intend using their graduations, look very closely before you buy them, to satisfy yourself that they are normal ones: some are made for pattern makers and carry 'stretched' measurement units to allow for contraction of the various metals upon removal from the casting mould.

Most try-squares are not as square on the outer edges as they are on the inner ones. Plastic stocks are usually accurate on both because the edges of the stocks can be machined parallel.

Spirit levels, like all reference tools, are only useful insofar as they remain accurate. To test a spirit level, place it on a known level surface. Take the reading and then turn the level around to see that it gives the same reading.

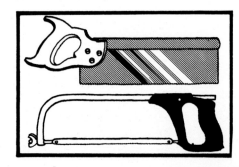

Marking and measuring

Steel tape rules provide the most helpful service. A good one will have a hook-end that slides to compensate for the tab thickness. If it did not, you would be that much out whenever you measured anything like a cupboard width for a shelf. It will also state the width of its case so that you can add this into a measurement if necessary.

Always mark wood with a knife or a gauge rather than a pencil. Knife lines are more precise, and the wood does not splinter across them. Scalpel or drawing knives are especially good for marking out, used with their low angle blades. If you want to do repairs involving mortice and tenon joints, get a combined gauge for parallel lines that will serve as an ordinary marking gauge as well.

Sawing

Hand-set saws are always easier to use. A junior hacksaw or a tenon saw should cope with most repairs, but before you buy a tenon saw, decide what kind of mitre box or sawing jig you want, if any. Some need larger saws than others.

Shaping and smoothing

To cut down hardened resin filler quickly, one of the milled files sold with special holders is invaluable, particularly if you need to cut the filler down in or near a corner. Triangular or rat's tail files are also essential — some rather clever ones, such as Abrafile, are now available. These files have soft cores, so you can bend them to any odd shape you need for inaccessible places.

File handles are normally sold separately from their working ends. When you choose your own handles, look for solid plastic ones, or the wooden safety type which have a metal coil incorporated to prevent the metal end of the file piercing the wood.

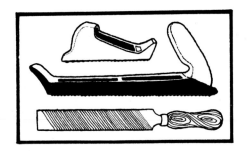

Chiselling

Although a chisel is probably the most efficient cutting tool in existence, it is also the most dangerous. Paradoxically, it is most potentially harmful when in least efficient condition, that is to say, when it is blunt.

The essential character of its edge is to be sharp, rigid and hard. Whatever force you put behind a chisel is distributed over this narrow cutting edge only. It should be kept razor-keen so that you never have to force it to do its work. Even when you hit the chisel with a mallet, to cut out a mortice for example, heavy blows should be totally unnecessary.

When properly sharpened, a chisel edge is bevelled only on the front; its back is kept absolutely flat to the oilstone to rub off the honing burr. This feature gives it the invaluable ability to cut exactly in line with its back. When working with a chisel always keep your eye on the back and not the axis of the handle. The two ought to be one and the same, but in practice they very rarely are.

Since you cannot keep your eye on two things at once, and you *must* keep it on the back alignment of the blade, only tap a chisel handle with the broad striking face of a mallet. If you use a hammer, you are very apt to slip and smash a finger or two.

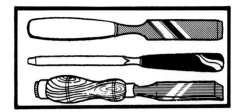

Drilling holes

Ordinary 'jobber's' drill twist bits are really designed for metal, but they will drill almost anything, except masonry. Being made to tight tolerances, they are good for making dowel-holes, especially in conjunction with a dowel jig. When drilling wood with them it is advisable to withdraw and clean any dust and bits out of the flutes every now and then. How far they will penetrate without sticking depends on the kind of wood.

There are special twist drills for wood which reduce in diameter towards the back more markedly than standard ones, but they are a little harder to find.

Ordinary auger bits may be up to a third of a millimetre ($\frac{1}{64}$-inch) in diameter bigger than the nominal size. For dowelling you will need the more accurate and therefore more expensive dowel bits, which tend to be a little short for use with dowel jigs.

Forstner bits need a steady hand, but produce usefully flat-bottomed holes. Guided by their cutting rim instead of by their point, they also come in handy for boring holes very near the edge of the wood. In this work it is easier to keep them straight if you have a ratchet brace.

Power drills need power-type bits, without screwed points and with extra-efficient chip clearance.

Masonry drills have tungsten carbide tips. This hard metal is made in several grades, but the tip hardness is not as important as the quality of the brazing between tip and drill body. Some will melt if you drill at over 1,000 rpm, while others will stand 3,000 with no protest. Bear in mind that single-speed drills normally turn at around 3,000 rpm.

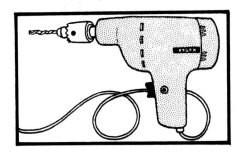

Screw driving

Wood screws are infinitely easier to use with screw-sink type pilot-hole bits, which make thread, shank and countersink-bevel preparation in one drilling. However, to get their full advantage you need a power drill. There is a different bit for each size and gauge of screw.

If you have to screw into chipboard, you will need to use special screws, such as the self-tapping ones. Ordinary ones do not get much of a grip in chipboard.

Ugly rust stains may appear in oak if you leave steel screws in it. This is because oak contains tannin which attacks the steel. Bright zinc-plated screws are better.

Planing

When planing surfaces on second-hand furniture, you may find that unseen nails or screws can chip the cutter edge of the plane, requiring it to be reground. The best general-purpose plane for unforeseen planing is one which has replaceable blades, such as the PTFE-coated planemaster type, with cheaply replaceable blades. These can rough down, smooth or rebate.

A small block plane for fine-finishing is also useful, preferably a $9\frac{1}{2}$, which has a mouth that can be closed up for work on curly grain.

Quick guide to adhesives

Animal glues are the traditional glues used by furniture makers. They are strong, quite flexible, but will not resist damp or heat. Scotch glue is an example.

PVA adhesives have generally superseded animal glues as the main adhesive for woodworking. They set in 20 minutes and dry in 24 hours.

Ureas are useful adhesives to use if you need to fill a gap and fix two things together (as with loose furniture joints).

Epoxy resins are the strongest and most versatile of the general-purpose glues. They are very good for mending glass and china as they are not affected by hot water.

Clear household adhesives are useful for most small, general repairs, but they are not especially strong. Do not use them on things subject to heat or hot water.

Natural latex is a tough, flexible adhesive designed for textile repairs. It will withstand washing in hot water, but not dry cleaning.

Rubber resin and synthetic latex adhesives will stick PVC tiles, rubber, and felt to concrete or hardboard. They will also join fabric, leather, ceramic tiles and reinforced plastic.

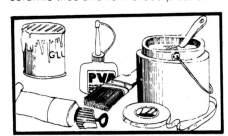

SIMPLE REPAIRS

Door and drawer locks (Fig. 1)

Having replaced worn, eroded or broken wood on the edge of a locking drawer or door, the lock-mortise chisel shown would be the best tool for re-cutting the mortise slot. This chisel is worked by striking it with a hammer, so it is possible to see exactly what you are doing. Cut the mortise by the 'crumbling' method shown. If you need to sink a plate, cut the housing out last.

Hinges (Fig. 2)

If the only fitting problem is filling in worn screw-holes, use small hardwood plugs chipped off with a chisel from a small, cross-cut piece of wood. Jam them in firmly behind the screws and sand down any protruding edges with abrasive paper.

When fitting hinges from scratch, mark all hinge positions by measuring from the same point, allowing for clearances (see right). A hinge's effective width is read at its thickest part, normally the pin, but look out for unusual types.

Broken legs and feet (Fig. 3)

Old breaks in ornamental legs or feet can rarely be repaired without some remaking. Fresh breaks in legs of any shape can be glued almost invisibly, but a connecting dowel is necessary for adequate strength.

To find the correct position for the dowel, tap a panel pin into one section of the break and file the end sharp. Press this end into the other section so that it marks where the dowel should go. Remove the pin and hand-drill a small hole in each part of the break. Use a drill bit the same diameter as the dowel, so that it will fit snugly into place. Chamfer the ends of the dowel and make a narrow groove along its length to allow excess glue to escape.

Broken or loose chair stretchers or rails (Fig. 4)

If you can match the timber, it is less trouble and takes less skill to replace a stretcher than to repair it. If you taper the tenons on the stretcher, you must 'spring' the leg joints as you slot in the tenons.

Broken or loose chair splats (Fig. 5)

It is usually possible to locate the top of the splat by looking for short dowels, or sometimes, sawn-off screws. When repairing, lever the bottom end into place before fixing it with dowels or screws which should be put in upwards through the lower rail of the chair back. This avoids visible repair scars and (provided the meeting surfaces are clean and well-glued) makes a firm fixing.

Burns or dents in solid tops (Fig. 6)

Ideally, you should remove a shallow burn mark by planing or sanding down the entire surface to the bottom level of the scraped-out depression. On a hardwood top, however, this would be too laborious and it is best to treat the hole only.

Most cigarette burns can be rubbed out of wood with a fine abrasive paper. A shallow burn can be coloured in with matching artist's oil paints and repolished when dry. Deep burns can be filled with coloured beeswax or epoxy resin. Fill burn holes in a French polished surface with a little semi-set polish. When dry, blend in the surface coat patch on top.

Dents in solid surfaces can usually be raised with a warm iron and a damp rag.

Local treament for blemishes

These treatments are only for minor or superficial blemishes.

Scratches can be remedied with pro-

prietary scratch removers or rubbed out with flour paper which has been dipped in linseed oil. Fill deep scratches with melted beeswax, coloured slightly darker than the surrounding surface. When it has nearly set, rub it into the crack, and repolish the surface as appropriate.

Heat marks appear as white patches on cellulose and lacquer finishes and on French polish.

Rub with a 1 to 1 mixture of real turpentine and linseed oil, or real turpentine and camphorated oil. Clean off with vinegar and repeat the process until the mark has gone. You may also use a proprietary ring remover.

Alcohol is a solvent which will soften most polishes, so wipe up spills immediately, and leave the surface to set. If the alcohol has removed the polish, rebuild the area with coloured French polish applied with a small brush. Then rub it first with flour paper which has been dipped in linseed oil, and next with a soft pad until it blends in with surrounding areas. Superficial spirit or heat marks on semi-matt finishes can be removed with fine steel wool, but to obtain an even surface, you may need to rub over the entire surface. Then rewax with furniture polish.

Black marks are usually caused by water which has seaped beneath the finish. To repair them, the finish must be removed. Oxalic acid crystals are then added to a cup of water until no more will dissolve (a saturated solution), and the mark is swabbed with this. Oxalic acid does not damage finishes, so it will safely remove superficial ink stains as well.

Dents, burns or bubbles on veneered tops (Fig. 7)

Dents that penetrate a veneer surface need a carefully matched patch set in – not an easy job. If, however, the dent is superficial, you can sand through the top surface until the criss-cross marks made by toothing planes on the base can *just* be seen. Then stop and refinish.

Bubbles in veneers are caused by glue failure. Find and cure the cause (damp, fungus, bleach) then nick the bubble along the grain with a pointed knife. Work more hot-melt Scotch glue under the surface with the same knife and press down carefully with a warm iron and a damp rag.

Sticking or sagging drawers (Fig. 8)

Sticking is usually caused by swollen wood – a product of damp. If this is the case, use chalk to establish exactly where the trouble is, then plane, shave or sand away the excess wood. Seal with oil or lacquer to stop more moisture from entering the drawer and drawer rail.

Gate leg tables: rule joints (Fig. 9)

The only reason for a good quality gate leg joint to stick or bind is failure of the finish to keep out moisture, which then swells the wood just enough to give trouble. Often, all you need do to cure it is to put the piece in a dry atmosphere for a few days. If this does not work, the hinge will have to be moved over about 2 mm ($\frac{1}{16}$ inch) to allow the flap free movement.

Panels split at the joins (Fig. 10)

Panels are not normally glued into their supporting grooves, but are left free to slide, so that the furniture will not warp under the strain of the wood shrinking with age. It is often possible to reglue joints between panel components, using temporary screws or pins at the back to wire or string them together until the glue sets. Use hot-melt, animal glue, compatible with the original glue.

Panels split in the grain (Fig. 11)

Since no great strength is demanded of panels, the pieces used for them are often short-grained in places. With age, they warp and can rarely be reglued. Narrow cracks can be disguised with appropriately coloured wood stopper (slightly darker than the raw wood). If the cracks are wide and you do not want to paint the wood, it may be necessary to replace the whole panel, but this is not an easy job.

Beading and moulding repairs (Fig. 12)

If you can match the old beading closely enough to be unnoticeable, it is preferable to replace complete sections rather than small portions. Often it is not possible to get a good match, in which case the damaged piece should be cut out so that the new wood can be 'keyed' in. Match the shape of the new wood to the original by using very narrow planes. Web clamps are helpful to secure the new piece when gluing it in place.

STRIPPED FINISHES

If you have decided that it is necessary to remove the old finish completely from a piece of furniture, you will find that you are faced with a choice of methods. Make it logically.

Look before you leap is a very sound adage in any context, but especially so where the shifting of old finishes is concerned. Difficult though it may be to guess what could be underneath an opaque coating, you should at the very least establish whether it is solid wood or veneer. (See page 66.) And by all means decide whether or not the piece can tolerate a complete stripping job — some solvents can be very hard on joints or on the wood itself. If you suspect that the piece, or perhaps just the finish alone, may be valuable, do not take any action without first taking expert advice.

Stripping methods

Chemical strippers are by far the easiest and most effective to use on furniture. Milder solutions will remove French polish (methylated spirit) or cellulose lacquers (ammonia), but it may make for peace of mind to use a proprietary chemical stripper suitable for the particular finish you want to remove. This way you shed all the will-it-won't-it worry and get clear and reliable instructions on what you need to do to remove residues. N.B. Strippers are strong chemicals, so take the obvious precaution against fumes, drips and skin contact. Should chemicals get on to your skin or in your eyes, rinse immediately with cold water.

Hard scraping to remove a finish will damage the wood but you should not have to do any, as the proper stripper will lift and soften the film for you. Thick or otherwise obstinate coverings sometimes need extra time for the chemicals to soak in or even additional applications of the stripper before any scraping is begun. Whenever the instructions offer a choice, wash the stripped wood with methylated spirit or a mineral turpentine substitute rather than water.

N.B. Some solvents will darken the wood, so again, it is always wise to do a patch test first. If you do not want the wood darkened, you will need to bleach it after stripping.

To bleach or not to bleach?

The main reasons for bleaching wood are to lighten the overall colour or to remove local staining, but you may

not need to bleach at all. A certain degree of natural variation in colour density, or shade differences between boards, can add to the honesty of appearance and give character to an ordinary piece of furniture.

What to bleach with

Ordinary domestic bleach is very dilute, far too mild for drastic work on wood. Stronger mixes of it can be made with crystals, but be careful to add crystals to water, NOT water to crystals. The reason for this lies in the heat which may be generated on contact; a small quantity of water could quickly boil and spit. Try to obtain pre-mixed bleach solutions whenever possible.

Sodium hypochlorite is very good for removing colour from wood, but if you have ink or iron stains to deal with, oxalic acid is better: about 100 grammes to a litre of water, if you buy it in crystal form. Always remember that, like most other bleaches, it is a first-class poison and a skin-stripper.

Two-part bleaches are the most powerful of all. They are very likely to attack the Scotch glue used for most joints and can lift veneers. Beware of using them.

Filling holes and cracks

Repairing a surface for opaque paints or lacquers is no trouble at all because you can use a variety of stopping compounds, not bothering about their colours. It is when you come to patch up blemishes for the finer, translucent varnishes, or for French polish, that complications set in.

Few, if any, fillers absorb stain or lacquer as readily as natural wood, so there is usually a need for some experimentation to secure a good blend of colour. The alternative techniques are to stain the stopping before you put it in or to use a ready-coloured kind, a bit darker than the surrounding wood.

Bruises in wood surfaces can be levelled up with a warm iron and a damp rag. Small scratches, dents or burns may not need a stopper covering if you are finishing with French polish. First, gently scrape out the damaged places to get a good key. Then allow the air to get to the requisite minute quantity of polish. Press it firmly into place as soon as it thickens and rub it level with fine abrasive paper when it is dry. The repair should be permanent and invisible, once polished over.

53 **Opposite: Some wood looks best left in its natural state. Protect the wood with a clear seal.**
Right: Some examples of stripped finishes. The settle has been fumed; the cupboard limed; and the chair stripped down to the natural wood.

Grain filling

This is nothing to do with damage, but with the wood's natural grain crevices, which must be filled in before you can varnish a surface. Unless you are to use a polyurethane covering, tint the grain filling compound to match the wood. This can be very tricky, usually involving powder colours ground in oil, so if you feel doubts turn to a transparent grain filler such as that made by Furniglas. However, do not use it under anything other than a polyurethane finish.

Liming

A specialized method of grain filling used to be applied to English oak to bring out the beauty of its grain. Possibly you may have to imitate the process, which consisted in bringing up the grain by wetting and/or wire brushing, scrubbing cream-thick lime solution into the pores with a cloth and rubbing the surface down with abrasive paper after it was dry. Be especially protective of eyes and hands.

Fuming

Another process used on oak was known as fuming; this darkened the wood from its natural light yellow colour. If you have to mend a fumed-oak piece with new wood, you will have to do the fuming before the new component is fitted.

Stand the item in an ammonia-proof drum or container, but do not allow it to touch the concentrated ammonia solution in the bottom. Remember that the chemical attacks some plastics, and that it isn't entirely kind to human beings. All the fumes do to the wood is darken it, so you do not need to bother about residues. Be sure always to work in a well-ventilated room.

STAINS, SEALS AND POLISHES

Very often after you have bleached and filled the wood for your piece, you may like to change the colour by applying a stain of some sort. To prevent any adverse reaction between the stain and a surface finish, try to use a stain which has been recommended by the manufacturer of the surface finish you intend to use.

Whether you have bleached the piece or not, the colour of the wood is bound to affect that of the stain you may want to dye it with. Always consider this when you are choosing colours and make a patch test just to be safe.

Occasionally, you may want to stain only a small area of a piece to match an existing stain. Proprietary matt stains are possible to use for this or you may make up your own stains to the specifications given below.

Mahogany. Bichromate of potash crystals dissolved in water will darken mahogany. Make a concentrated solution and dilute it as required, always testing on a hidden spot before committing yourself. The stain darkens as it dries, so allow the test patch to dry out before proceeding.

Oak. Vandyke crystals dissolved in water with a little ammonia 880 will make an oak stain.

Bismark brown makes a red stain which is useful for warming up other stains.

Black aniline dye is the best for retouching ebony.

To apply the stain, use a soft, dry cloth or a medium-sized brush and apply a coat of the stain evenly over the entire piece. To ensure even colouring, wipe any excess with a clean cloth before the stain dries.

Any kind of stain is safe under oil, but if you want a brilliantly coloured stain water-alcohol borne types, such as those made by Dylon, are the ones to use under modern, chemically curing finishes. All of these dyes are quite simple to use. Remember, however, that they raise grain, so you need to damp surfaces, rub flat with fine abrasive paper when dry and then put the stain on, all *before* you attempt the final surface lacquer or polish.

Surface applications
Before you decide what kind of finish to apply to old wood, consider carefully whether or not its present surface holds any visual or tactile charm that is better preserved than lost.

Transparent varnishes and lacquers are rarely worth leaving, but perhaps you have a piece of furniture that has been finished in the fashion of the pre-French polish era: sealed with linseed oil and repeatedly waxed. This way of protecting a surface is effective for any item unlikely to be subjected to abuse by heat or abrasion and the years of elbow-grease expended on it provide a soft, lustrous patina impossible to replace.

Oiled and waxed finishes
If you plan on conserving such a finish, the prescription is simply more of the same medicine. Take the wax off by rubbing gently with a mineral turpentine substitute on cotton wool; wipe with a dry rag. Finally use linseed oil to reseal the surfaces.

Boiled linseed oil is thicker and more treacly than raw, but you may use either – diluted up to 50/50 with a mineral turpentine substitute if you want to avoid darkening the timber's colour. Even with the diluted oil, you should apply a series of very thin coats with a rag or soft brush, letting each coat dry before putting more on. Continue the oil feeding until the wood will not absorb any more, then rub hard with a clean rag to remove any excess there may be. Use a hard wax, massaged to a shine with grade 000 steel wool to complete the finish.

If you prefer you may use teak oil for this process; it dries quicker than linseed oil and is more resistant to marking.

Resistant finishes
Old wood that has been stripped, perhaps even mildly bleached to remove stains, may still be quite reasonably attractive. To enhance and protect its good looks, you need only give it a careful rub with fine glasspaper and three or four coats of a modern synthetic lacquer.

All transparent finishes darken natural wood to some extent, but if you especially want to avoid any hint of golden brown, use a catalyzed clear lacquer rather than a polyurethane. Lacquers of this kind (Furniglas Hardset is a good example) are just as tough as polyurethanes, but, unlike polyurethanes, cannot be stored once the catalyst has been added. A widely unappreciated feature of catalyzed finishes is that you can put thin, smooth coats on top of basic brush coats with a pad.

Polyurethane practice
Polyurethanes are only as tough as their reputation if they are applied directly to the wood surface – anything coming between may affect their performance. Unlike oils, they will not soak into wood so, to get firm adhesion, dilute the first coat 50/50 with the makers' recommended solvent and the second with 25 per cent solvent. Regard these as a preparation for the three or four full-strength coats necessary. Rub down lightly between coats with 320 or finer grit abrasive paper, or with 000 steel wool.

For a perfect surface
Although modern lacquers can attain an extremely high gloss surface finish by brushing, spraying or pad polishing, there is always the chance of making blemishes with embedded dust or hair – these are almost impossible to avoid with the comparatively long drying time. This is where French polish scores over polyurethanes; its essential quality is the speed at which it sets, drying almost as soon as it leaves the pad, and enabling it to be applied free of inclusions. This very useful virtue has made it traditionally a master craftsman's prerogative to apply – a high degree of skill being needed to get a clean finish, free of smear and bloom.

Two versions of proprietary French polish, such as those made by Furniglas, now overcome this difficulty by means of a special chemical finishing solution. You simply wipe it on after pad polishing, then off again to eliminate those pad marks which used to give apprentices to the trade nightmares.

If you intend to French polish over a polyurethane or catalyzed lacquer, choose a proprietary polyurethane version, but do not attempt to apply this one over ordinary French polish because the under layer of the combined finish will still be heat sensitive. The standard grade is the better one for repairing or reviving the traditional shellac-based finishes. Usually a cleaning fluid is provided to be used with both kinds of polish.

54 Opposite above: Use natural wood stains to enhance the grain or colour of a piece. Avoid staining woods such as mahogany, walnut or maple. Notice the reflection in the French polished surface of the right hand side of the lower table. Opposite below: Try staining with water-alcohol fabric dyes or artist's inks, as well as normal coloured wood stains.

PAINTING IT PLAIN

Sound, solid and utilitarian though your selected secondhand furniture may be, a high proportion of it is bound to be made from wood with an indifferent surface. Instead of using a clear finish which only produces a disappointing renovation, imagine such pieces straight-painted. They may prove to compare favourably with relatively featureless modern items — whereas if you tried to give them a pretentious finish you might draw attention to their shortcomings.

Superfine painting

Paint is essentially a cosmetic, so to ensure a flawless finish you must have a good foundation. Not too many years ago, it would have been necessary to strip or scrape any surface back to the bare wood, so that you could fill securely and sand finely to get the necessary smooth and unbroken surface. If you have to go to these lengths to get rid of the old finish, any proprietary pre-paint filler will give you an acceptable fair surface to start on. If you have not stripped so thoroughly, the finer fillers close the grain better and may, in the end, save you an extra coat of paint.

Sanding smooth and flat

A thousand laborious ways can be found to get a surface ready for perfectionist painting. One of them is to trowel in a fine filler, then proceed to gouge it out with coarse-grit abrasive paper. All the 60 to 100-grit abrasive work should be done before the filler is put in, leaving as little raised above the surface as possible. Successive rubbings with 150-grit and 320-grit grades will then leave the base you want.

Enemies of adhesion

Before you pick up the paint pot, think back to reassure yourself that no residues are left in the wood which might tend to lift or discolour the new paint film. Possible invisible lurkers are oil, grease, wax, stripping/bleaching/washing compounds, resinous knots and, last but not least, water. Provided you have washed the wood down thoroughly and have allowed it to dry out before filling, only knots should be liable to give trouble; it is always a good idea to seal them off with patent knotting solution and (on softwoods) to use an aluminium primer, which is not the colour of aluminium, but contains a compound of the metal that is very good at resisting the penetration of resin.

More about sanding

Abrasive paper will only cut down bumps on flat sections or remove splinters in hollows if it is supported so that it conforms to the contours of the surface you are working on. Often only your fingertips can be used to hold the paper, although small pieces rolled up can be better to work into narrow flutes and mouldings.

Flat surfaces and edges alike should be block-sanded, the abrasive supported by a flat wooden 'brick', a cork rubbing-pad or a patented hand-sanding holder. If you use special steel-backed sanding sheets, be very careful not to put tucks in them when you fold them into the holder because the resulting corners can make ugly gouge marks.

Power tools

Orbital or rotary-powered sanding tools can be both labour-saving and effective on flat surfaces, but none are really good enough to use on curved parts for fine work. Even with extreme care, flexible disc sanders or attachments for power drills are likely to hollow out a flat section. Instead try using a rigidly backed rotary device or even better, a proper orbital sander. Avoid orbital pads that are not stable. Some simply waggle vigorously around a central pivot, whereas the gentle, scrubbing action of the 'eccentrically' driven kind gives a proper finish.

Without doubt self-powered machines are more effective than attachments for electric drills, because they are made for a single purpose. Either way, it's as well to remember that a sander is a finishing tool and should not be used for heavier work.

There is no point in using any grit coarser than 100 for an orbital pad. Whichever grit you start with, 100 or finer, you will get the best results by working steadily through the available grades up to 320 or 400-grit for the final finish.

Final precautions

Contra-indications are not so much don'ts as nevers: Never add any of your weight (however slight) to that of the sander itself and never cover any of the motor's air vents with either hand. An orbital sander's jobs tend to be long, so the motor needs all the cooling air it can get. Work in slow loops, not straight down the grain, never letting your sander rest with the motor running.

Never tip either end or side when in motion, or allow the pad to touch adjacent walls or ledges. Never stop short of unobstructed edges, nor let the pad project more than an inch or so beyond them.

When you get to the final, finest grade of abrasive paper, carefully and evenly hold the sander as if to lift it bodily straight into the air, but keep it very lightly in contact with the wood.

If you have decided to leave the existing finish on and paint over it, do all but the finest sanding, wipe the dust away and use a spackle (e.g. a cellulose filler, such as Fine Surface Polyfilla) to fill in holes and dents, including those in the old coating. Then fine-sand and proceed to undercoat.

Priming and undercoating

From now on, be clean. Ideally you will have taken off all removable fittings and vacuumed away all dust. Clean the floor while you are at it, close the doors and windows to keep out dust, smoke and insects. If you are a smoker, give it up for safety's sake while you are in the paint room. Wrap up long hair. Leave hairy or woolly clothes in the wardrobe.

To get the best possible paintwork it's worth investing in the best brushes you can afford. Thin, flat, chisel-tip brushes are a great temptation to the inexperienced because they look so manageable. However, when full of paint some of the really inexpensive ones do about as good a job as an old sponge.

The better brushes are fat, with fine, silky bristles that both hold a good charge of paint and spread it out at an even rate. They work with a firm, springy touch like that of an old-fashioned pen nib. The firmness lets you work with the bristle tips.

Between coats

As soon as each coat of paint is thoroughly dry, rub it down with extreme gentleness, using 500 grit, or finer, abrasive paper. In this way you get rid of any odd particles and hairs which may have landed on the surface during drying, and make a sound base for the following top-coats.

With these later coats be as stingy with the paint as it will let you, short of taking it off again. Remove dust between every coat. For heavy-wearing use, substitute an extra gloss topcoat for one of the undercoats.

55 **Opposite: A few coats of paint can transform any dingy piece into a cheerful addition to the home.**
Above left: Brighten up a nursery by converting an old washstand into a baby's dresser, with a thorough clean inside and out and a colourful painted finish.
Above right: If a bargain piece looks ungainly and drab, strip off the original finish, paint it a brilliant colour and make a feature of its nooks and crannies by lining them with complementary paper or fabric.
Below: Gloss paints are excellent for tables and chairs: they are easy to wipe clean and the paint protects the wood against nicks and scrapes.

DECORATIVE DESIGNS AND STENCILS

For renovators who have found in the process of plain painting that they have a clear eye and a steady hand, contrasting features painted on to an old piece of furniture can completely transform its character. With a bit of planning and imagination, you can make an undistinguished collection of sticks and panels the centre of attention and interest.

Freehand picture patterns

If you make a panel or other chosen section a light coloured oasis in a dark desert of plain paint, the very fact of its colourful existence will draw more attention than any minor imperfections of execution. Pictures on common articles of household furniture are so little encountered, especially on modern furniture designs, that you are far more likely to be congratulated for enterprise than criticized for your specific talents. And moreover, you do not have to be an artistic genius to paint respectable designs. Copying and tracing are both quite legitimate methods of providing yourself with a theme or a shape.

Choosing the paint

Assuming that you start with an object stripped bare of all previous finishes and completely prepared for repainting, you must first decide on the type of paint you want to use. This will enable you to choose the correct primer: aluminium-based ones for softwoods; almost any lead-free type for hardwoods (diluted with a mineral turpentine substitute in the proportions recommended by the manufacturer); and none at all if you are applying a pure polyurethane final finish. The best primer for this type of finish is an eggshell from the same range: dilute the first coat with 50 per cent mineral turpentine substitute and the second with 25 per cent. This will help to make the polyurethane sink into the surface as deeply as possible.

Guide to painting

Let your approach to painting be governed first of all by the contrast between your ground and the pattern or picture background. If the contrast is strong you will probably find it easier to paint the entire object and then superimpose your design onto the background. If there is little contrast, you may prefer to leave a bare wood patch for the design. In this case, when the ground colour is to be brushed or sprayed on, simply mark out the area you need to leave unpainted with chalk or a felt pen and follow the line as closely as you can with a fine brush. Should the area be a complex or difficult shape itself, you may have to trace it from your original. Once you have copied the outline on to your tracing paper, you can shade the underside with a very soft pencil. Put the tracing on to the wood and rub along the lines to press them through.

When the ground colour is to be applied you will need to have some form of protective masking. Self-adhesive vinyl coverings, such as Fablon or Contac, are very effective when stuck on to hardened paint surfaces. They may, however, leave residues on bare wood which will give trouble later. Of course, you can always ensure that no spots of adhesive remain by rubbing the bare patch with a rag moistened with surgical spirit (rubbing alcohol).

Masking solution

Certain types of special 'masking solutions', such as Humbrol's Maskol, have now been specifically developed to eliminate harmful adhesive residues. Painted thinly on the reserved area before you apply the ground, it dries in about 15 minutes to a thin, flexible, rubbery film. If you seal into it a small piece of paper or card, you can peel the protected patch off cleanly when the last spray-coat has dried thoroughly.

Fablon masking precautions

Since PVC coverings (Fablon or Contac) are not designed especially for masking, it is essential that the ground colour is thoroughly hard-dry before putting the mask in place. This means letting alkyd paints dry for at least four days and polyurethanes for a week. An exact shape can be cut with the PVC peel-off backing still in place, leaving you a clean outline with a hard edge to paint around.

Stencilling

For people whose self-confidence and enterprise falls short of attempting original or freehand-copied artwork, there are other ways of bringing life and variety to painted articles.

Stencilling is perhaps the simplest to do, even though the process requires more than average care. Whether you spray or brush through the cutouts, the chief risk is of paint seeping under an unsecured edge.

PVC materials can be used to make stencils, in much the same way as for masking. To prevent the paint from lifting when you remove the self-adhesive material, allow several days for the ground colour to dry before applying the stencil.

Stick-ons and slide-ons

Yet another method of decorating a plain surface is to use any of the ready-made self-adhesive motifs available. They are especially effective on furniture in children's rooms or playrooms.

Beware, however, that the pictures will be slightly raised from the surface they are applied to and so need careful application to be sure that the edges do not roll up. Occasionally, you will find odd projections on some of these designs, where an animal's tail sticks out for example, so it pays to loosen the figure from its backing all around the edges before you stick it down by the approved method — peeling the backing off gradually as you smooth the design down.

Since the adhesive on the back of most of these motifs is now non-drying, you will find that you can take them off cleanly even after some years. Occasionally you may get a small obstinate patch left on, but this should be easy to remove with surgical spirit (rubbing alcohol) or toluene (a common dye solvent).

Transfers

Supreme thinness is the outstanding virtue of a transfer, which consists of colour printed on to a thin, transparent film which has a water-soluble, gelatinous backing. Although you can slide it about a bit after soaking the backing off and slipping the picture on to the surface, remember that it is fragile and can be pulled apart with the slightest clumsiness. Once in place and dry, however, it becomes part of the surface. A coat of clear, acid-hardening lacquer will protect it.

56 Opposite: For an imaginative touch, add more than plain colour to your favourite furniture.
Above left: A sunny yellow dresser decorated with simple white stars and clouds echoes the wallpaper's colours.
Above right: A basic rectangular shape such as this chest looks good with the legs removed and a central front panel painted in an abstract design.
Below: Large panelled items are usually ideal for painting in several colours and decorating with repeated patterns.

Ideas for design

Inspiration for designs can come from almost anywhere. Nature has always been a source of ideas for pictorial borders and motifs — flowers, animals, patterns, all can be found there. Old books can also be a terrific source of unusual imagery. Some people might find inspiration in needlework patterns as well. And in addition to pictures or designs, consider lettering as an unusual alternative.

Whatever pictures or patterns that you do choose to decorate a plain panel or border edge, be sure that the design is of a similar, compatible style to the piece of furniture. For example, delicate curves and bold regular, geometric patterns are, as a rule, not a good mixture. Also be sure that the size of your design is in proportion to the area that you are painting on. As a final precaution, keep in mind the use to which you are going to put the object.

Colour sense

As with all techniques for renovating furniture, the inexperienced should always try out their ideas first to be sure that they work. Colour combinations are no exception. Probably the most important thing to remember is that complementary colours will enhance one another — to make a colour more prominent put it next to its complement (blue-orange, yellow-purple, red-green). Also any glaze which is put on to a painted surface will usually soften the colours.

Stripes

Plain stripes are the most effective treatment for certain types of furniture. You will find that they are easiest to apply if you use a flat, narrow brush, or even better one of the brushes specially made for striping (ask at your local art supply shop or a good DIY shop).

When painting, be sure that the paint is thin enough to flow easily from the brush and that you put plenty of paint on it. Let the brush move along smoothly: little pressure from your hand is needed. If you lift the brush up in the middle of the stripe it is almost certain to show. Once again, practice will be the best instructor. A straight-edge is always a useful guide to keep handy. If you are doing corner stripes, make the lines go just beyond the corner point and wipe off the excess immediately. Work carefully and at a fairly quick pace — too slow and the shakes will show.

Experiment

Besides design and colour you might try experimenting a bit with special effect paints, such as glitter or metallic paints. Be sparing with their application, as a touch is usually enough to create the desired look.

For unusual textures you might also try applying one of the many coloured glazes now on the market, with feathers, rough cloth or paper.

Freehand techniques

Only a fortunate few will be able to paint an original design directly on to the wood surface. Less gifted people will need help to make their imaginative visions look reasonably proficient. Perhaps the most helpful and encouraging way to show what can be achieved by tracing and copying, will be to describe how the rocking chair and sea-chest were done.

The Boston rocker

If there is any golden rule for design painting, it is to wait until the initial colour is bone-hard dry before proceeding to the next one. This is exactly how a watercolourist works to avoid blurred outlines.

Both the white ground and the tan border around the design on the chair were painted using PVC masks. The leaf shapes were achieved by tracing around a pattern with a piece of chalk and then painting in with fine, sable brushes. For almost any painted design work, sable brushes are the best to use. They have finely pointed

tips and round, seamless, non-corrodible ferrules. Sizes are denoted by numbers, each number relating to the diameter at the narrow end of the ferrule which holds the soft bristles. They range from No.1 at 1·65mm to No.10 at 6·45mm, so any fine work you need to do can be completed with a brush appropriate to the job. Without proper brushes, you do not give yourself a reasonable chance of success.

All veins and shading in the leaves were painted with a No. 3 brush – the veins in black enamel, diluted with a lot of mineral turpentine substitute

(proportions not critical) and the shading with the same brush but an even more dilute mixture of the colour.

Sea-chest design
One or two fatter pencils proved useful in the creation of the ship picture but no great art was involved. Since the imprecise rope border had been planned before the centre panel was painted, the panel outline was traced instead of masked. After priming the bare wood, the complete ship was traced on to it.

Sky was stippled in, then the green middle tint of the sea. The hull needed

a little reinforcement with a 7B pencil before it was painted in, and then the masts and sails were added.

Shading with a mixture of cream and white came next, then the darker green of the sea, the ropes and other fine details before the final 'white horses' and rope border.

57 Opposite above: A sea-chest design for a blanket box. To get the best effects, mix colours. Opposite below: Simple shapes can be traced on with everyday household templates. Above: A unique Boston rocker.

58 This page: Designs for the Boston rocker, the Tyrolean chest, the sea chest and an appealing rag doll for a child's room, are given as a guide for making accurate tracings and stencils. To enlarge a design from a small original, simply trace it up on a squared graph drawn to the scale of the proposed picture.

If using stencils, hold them firmly in place with masking tape; provide extra borders if using an aerosol spray paint. Test the masking tape on an unnoticeable area of a pre-painted base to be sure it does not pull off the paint.

PAINTING DIFFICULT SURFACES

Man-made boards make very sound replacements for tops too senile for renovation, but their edges may give rise to some trouble unless they are properly treated. Both blockboard and plywood edges show end grain, which absorbs paint to a greater extent than the rest of the wood. If you apply a thick coating of a cellulose filler, let it dry and then rub it down finely, the board's structure will become a close secret, after painting.

Chipboard edges should really be lipped with some smooth material for the best results, but the same treatment works quite well for their raw edges, too. Chipboard has a very abrasive texture, especially at the edges, which tends to tear abrasive paper, even if it is wrapped around a block. Steel-backed abrasive sheets, such as those supplied for some types of hand sanders are one solution to this problem.

Finally, unless you have one of the extra-fine surfaced chipboards, you will find that the broad surfaces need a certain amount of filling as well before you can paint them satisfactorily.

Spackling sound paint

Paradoxically, until recently dents and bruises in sound paintwork could be too shallow to fill, and so more difficult to hide than deep gouges or splits. Adhesive spackles, such as the vinyl-based Fine Surface Polyfilla, have changed all this. They are fine-textured enough to sand flush to the edges of the most gently undulating depression in painted wood (or painted anything). An additional advantage is that they need no primer, as they do not have the same tendency as ordinary filler to soak up the undercoat.

Painting plastics

Plastics are so many in kind and so various in character that it is nearly impossible to state rules of thumb concerning the sort of paint which can safely be used on any particular one. Any given plastic may react to a paint quite differently in one form than it does to the same paint when it has been made by a different method. Generally speaking, hard plastics can usually be painted safely with products that use a mineral turpentine substitute as their solvent. The only reliable guide to test the stability of the partnership is to try a little paint on an unobtrusive part of the plastic. Polyurethane paints are among the safest to try, and some spray paints, such as Humbrol aerosols, are safe to use even on expanded polystyrene.

59 Above: Plastic surfaces can be given striking new looks although they do present some difficulties for the painter. Always experiment beforehand to find the right paint: one which will not eat into the surface. Remember to plan ahead for matching designs and use masking tape or templates for accuracy.

THE KNACK OF APPLYING 'FAKE' FINISHES

Paints and surface finishes may be used to achieve effects which in no way resemble ordinary paintwork. If you are unable to find, or to afford, one of the more unusual types of material such as marble, malachite, ebony or a beautifully grained wood, it is possible to emulate them quite easily, with paint and paintbrush.

Sometimes the effect can be quite startling – and often pleasantly surprising. It is an especially good technique to use on fairly small or oddly shaped items which would be quite charming, except for their dull finish. A bit of practice and a good eye can produce imitations of expensive timbers, marbles or malachite which will deceive all but the expert. The main reason for applying faked finishes is, of course, to brighten an object's appearance by giving it an original surface, rather than to deceive.

The basics of deception
Whether you are graining to imitate wood or veining to imitate minerals, the basic technique is the same. First, a ground colour in an oil-based paint is put on and allowed to dry very well. A thin coat of linseed oil is applied on to this ground, using a soft pad to wipe it over, and various combinations of paint, or stain. Features can be added in two ways: either by removing part of the overlay or by painting them in with small brushes. Finally the design is sealed in with a clear varnish.

The most difficult aspects are getting the colours right and putting the features in, but with a little practice, any reasonably steady hand can produce quite effective results. The indispensable part of the process is a careful study of the material you are trying to recreate. If you cannot have it in front of you while you work, at least go and look at it for a good long time before you start.

For clear varnishing, acid-catalyzed lacquers, such as Furniglas Hardset, are better than polyurethanes. They do not have the slight brown tinge that is inseparable from the polyurethanes (fine for natural wood; death to light shades of paint).

The art of ebonizing
To give wood a solid, dense black appearance, with no grain figure visible whatsoever, you can use either a proprietary French polish preparation or a catalyzed lacquer to which you add black powder colour especially formulated for the job. Use the proportions recommended by the makers,

allowing several hours for the colour to dissolve. If the lacquer is a two-solution, catalyzed lacquer you need to add the hardener to the blackened lacquer just before using it.

Several brush coats go on before you start to pad-polish (preferably wearing rubber gloves). In this operation, you can have the best of both worlds by pad-polishing over the brush-coated lacquer with the blackened French polish preparation. If you do this, the surface will be easy to repair if it is scratched or dented. At the same time you will retain the heat and solvent protection of the base layers of catalyzed lacquer.

Graining the hat boxes
Even if you are only having fun with imitation surfaces, the effect would be marred by edges out of line or pronounced dents in the surfaces. The first priority in graining the hat boxes shown was to knock out the depressions and straighten up the edges. For both operations, the *light* hammering was done against a firm wood backing of appropriate shape.

After cleaning and degreasing with steel wool and a mineral turpentine substitute, the tinplate was given two undercoats, Marders Matsire MU2 for

the pine coloured box and MU4 for the rosewood one.

The next application is a very thin layer of oilpaint over a darker one, which is known as scumble. This was thinned down to the right shade with a two-to-one mixture of a mineral turpentine substitute and raw linseed oil, and was put on extremely thinly. All the grain lines were done with fine sable brushes, but if you can get any of the special graining tools the job will be even quicker and easier.

Large art supply firms still make pencil overgrainers for the annual-ring lines, mottlers which dig through scumble to make fine highlights, floggers for suggesting pores and softeners to blend the sharp lines a little and so reduce the artificiality.

Polyurethane varnish will not be as hard-wearing over the oil-based graining as it would be on its own, but it is still the best protection available.

60 Opposite: The grained boxes were done with artist's paints; the malachite box was painted with household paints and given two coats of a clear polyurethane finish tinted with green stain. Malachite and marble patterns shown below.

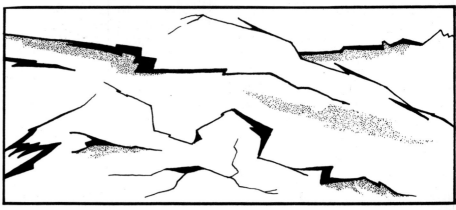

CANE FURNITURE

Bamboo is a giant grass plant, whereas rattan and malacca are slender stems from different kinds of palm tree. All are sometimes referred to as 'cane', to complete our confusion.

In practical terms this is of little consequence, because they all have rather similar characteristics. The difference between ordinary, tree-grown woods and the endogenous woody stems of the 'canes' is that, instead of forming new tissue on the outside as they grow, grasses and palms make their new growth on the inside. Notwithstanding this peculiar habit, endogens, of course, must have hollow stems. For this reason, they present us with hard, horny material on the outside, but with little or nothing on the inside to take screws, nails or any of the usual carpentry-orientated fastening devices.

Which is used for what
Although technically a grass, bamboo is normally used for furniture in a thicker and sturdier state of development than that made from palm stems such as rattan. The reason for this is that its segments tend to be longer, linked by rather knotty joints. Palms, on the other hand, have shorter, less irregular segments, with neater and smoother joins between them, which allow them to bend more readily into curves.

Problems in the spring
Although malacca (a favourite for walking-style canes) and rattan are ready to bend, they are equally ready to spring back straight again as soon as they are released from tension. When load-bearing furniture is made from these materials, this resilience has to be used to provide the resistance to deformation that solid timber gives through its natural stiffness.

By far the most usual method of fastening stems together is to bind them with thin strips of fibrous reed or cane. The binding strips will have been soaked in water to make them conform to the tight curves required in lashing rattan members together. Once in place and tied off (normally by being tucked under), the strips harden and become brittle.

Dealing with disintegration
Palm-built furniture very rarely comes apart because of longitudinal splits in the cane structural pieces. More often than not it is the bindings that break their bands and demand attention

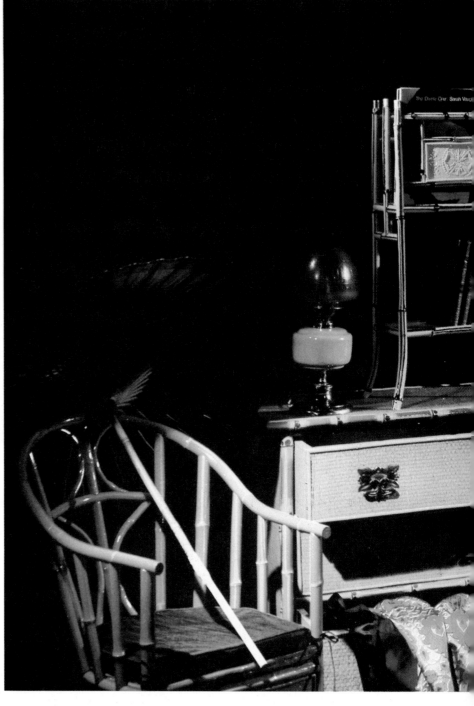

before the entire piece collapses.

Two problems arise when this happens. The original bindings cannot be re-used, and the bent members show a reluctance to go back to their original form. They, like the bindings, tend to increase in brittleness with age, so you may not be able to heave them into position quite so enthusiastically as the original maker did. A pan full of boiling water can work wonders in this situation. Be sure, however, that the water can drain away and that you can get the recalcitrant rod into place and lashed down before it again becomes set in its ways. 'Pea-stick' bamboo or split cane is best to use for any binding.

Bigger bamboos
Furniture made from the fatter and thicker walled bamboos may be held together by methods other than binding. To repair items that have been notched or pinned is perhaps easier than bandaging up the lashed-construction kind, because the big-diameter poles can, with care, be drilled — with care meaning with a power drill and a proper wood auger. Ordinary twist bits for drills tend to split the bamboo walls, as do hand auger bits, which have a screw-threaded point.

Screws can even be used, although you might need to fill part of a hollow stem with cellulose filler, such as Polyfilla, or one of the resin fillers used for repairing minor damage on car bodies. If you use the latter, it is advisable to drill it after it has set, inserting a masonry plug to give the screw a solid hold. Always drill at a slow speed to avoid splits and fractures.

Camouflaging the repair

It is inadvisable to bury screw heads below the bamboo surface, since you will need the full thickness of the wall to stop the screw from pulling through. If you must leave the screw flush with the surface, it can easily be disguised by a dab of paint.

Most of the repairs to bamboo or rattan furniture will, however, be rebinding jobs. Original strips will almost never be serviceable enough to be used again. And substitutes like plastic, string or plastic-covered wire can be disguised only by painting, fortunately a very effective rejuvenation treatment for this kind of furniture and one with a variety of possibilities.

Painting peculiarities

Whether laced together or notched and spiked, cane-constructions are bound to present more complex surfaces to be cleaned and painted than solid wood ones. For this reason, avoid powdery scouring compounds. Rely rather on strong-action liquid detergents, which can more reliably be washed out from the interstices and crannies. Pre-paint preparations are most effective, and can normally be let down to thinner solutions for simply lifting dirt. If you do intend painting or varnishing, use them at the recommended full strength.

Some pieces will respond to gentle cleaning with an old paintbrush, but others may need the stiffer persuasion of a scrubbing brush, for example. Sanding is naturally out of the question for all but the broadest bamboos, so it will help a lot if you can find a cleaner with an etching action thrown in to give paint a good key.

61 Above: Bamboo and rattan are remarkably versatile: cane chairs, tables, even chests of drawers, bring an interesting touch of the orient to a living room or bedroom. Liven up a narrow hallway with a spiky bamboo hallstand. Use an aerosol spray paint for awkward shapes and fine struts, or clean the cane and varnish it to show off its natural grain and colour.

While repairs to cane furniture such as bamboo and rattan may sometimes be awkward and the results uncertain, complete recaning of a simple chair seat or screen is a project well worth the effort. Even pieces with little or no value can be converted into attractive, useful additions to your home.

Buying cane

Cane can be bought at most craft or DIY shops and usually comes in bundles large enough to cover a small chair seat. There are six thicknesses identified by number. A normal-sized chair seat should be covered with grade four cane. Finishing work on the chair will require a small amount of grade two cane.

Preliminary steps

If you are recaning a damaged chair or article, begin by stripping off the old cane and discarding any pegs or nails which have been used to jam pieces of cane into the holes.

If you are caning a chair frame for the first time, you will need to drill holes for the cane. It is very important for the frame to be level all the way around. The holes must be drilled at the same spacing all round the frame — except where corners make this impossible. The centre front hole must line up exactly with the centre rear one and the side holes must line up exactly across the frame. Since chair frames are wider at the front than at the back, there will be more holes at the front, but this is not a problem.

For grade four cane, use a 3·00mm (⅛-inch) drill bit. Space the holes at 15mm (½-inch) between centres.

Clean out all holes — old or new — with a very fine wire or stick. Failure to do this may mean that the cane will stick. Also give the frame a quick wipe over with a mineral turpentine substitute and polish it if necessary.

Finally soak the cane to be used in cold water for at least five minutes so that it is pliable enough to work with. Repeat this while caning, if it becomes stiff.

Tools

The only tools you will need are three or four blunt pegs, made from thin dowels, to jam into the holes and hold the cane firm, and a razor blade.

Weaving the cane

Carefully study the weaving diagram at every stage of work. Begin with one strand of the softened cane, sharpened at both ends with the razor blade. Find the centre back and front holes and insert one end of the cane through the centre back hole, leaving about 25mm (1 inch) protruding below the underside of the frame. Jam a wooden peg into this hole to hold the cane firmly. Take the other end of the cane across to the centre front hole and push it through the hole from above. Be sure not to twist the cane; keep the shiny side upwards.

Pull the free end of the cane down through the frame so that it does not sag across the chair. Do not pull it too taut, since the cane will shrink as it dries. Pull the cane up through one of the holes adjacent to the centre front

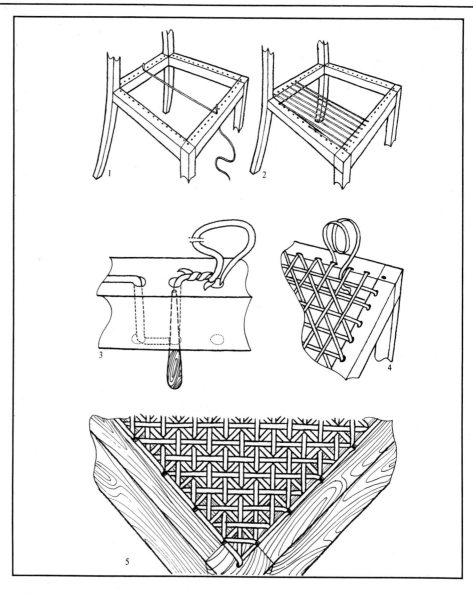

1. Begin caning from a hole at the back of the frame and secure the cane with a peg as shown.
2. With more holes in the front than the back, some strands will run from the front to a side hole.
3. Join a new length by looping it around the old and pulling it tight up through the next hole.

4. Diagonal canes must be interwoven with existing strands. After caning diagonally in one direction, apply the same method in the other.
5. Follow this weaving pattern for the seat at every stage. Figure 3 shows how the cane is passed from hole to hole.

one and back across the frame to the opposite hole, next to the centre back one. Continue to insert parallel strands across the top of the frame, joining lengths of cane as described below, until you reach the last hole before one of the rear corners.

Corners

Since there are more holes in the front than the back of the frame some strands will have to run from the front to a side hole. Be sure to place the strands so that they are kept exactly parallel to one another. When you have finished one side, return to the centre of the frame and work out to the other side; be sure to do both sides exactly the same.

Side to side

Begin at the front of the frame and string the cane from side to side. Lay the side to side canes over the front to back ones to provide a frame for the diagonally woven strands.

Diagonal strands

Study the weaving diagram carefully at every stage. Begin at either rear corner and pass the strand of cane over and then under the first two intersections of the strung cane. This will make the angle 45° to either of the first two sets of cane. String right across the frame to the corner, passing above and below alternate intersections. String the next diagonal piece of cane opposite to this one (over where you went under) and continue alternating each strand. Finish the weaving by stringing across the other diagonal, passing the strand below the intersections that the previous diagonals passed above. When you have finished, there will be three pieces of cane through each of the holes in the frame, except at the corners.

Joining pieces
Remember, when you are joining pieces of cane that it can only be done under the frame on the short stretch where the cane passes from one hole to another. Pass the first cane down through its hole and hold it firm at the top with a peg. Then loop, do not knot, the new piece around the protruding end, right up against the frame. Sharpen both ends of the new piece of cane and pass it up through its hole. Pull it tight and the looped link should jam up against the frame. This joint will hold when the cane dries. Remove pegs when a second piece of cane is passed through a hole.

Finishing off
When the cane dries, it shrinks in its holes and, therefore, may slip when a person sits on the seat. This can be avoided by the use of a cane reinforcement made of grade two cane. Begin with this thinner piece of cane and pass it up a frame hole from the underside.

Loop the piece around the three strands coming out of the top of the hole, and pass it down through the same hole. Then, take this piece along the underside of the frame to the next hole and repeat the procedure. This should be done all around the frame, joining up new lengths as previously described.

Finally, the edge of the seat may be decorated with more cane, preferably of a thick grade such as number six, threaded all around the edge of the frame in straight lines from hole to hole, as shown in the weaving diagram. To cover all the spaces between the holes you will need to go around the frame twice.

Basketweave and wickerwork
Though essentially different from furniture made from cane components lashed together, wickerwork constructions produce similar problems if they are badly broken. In fact, it would be wise to reconsider before buying a severely damaged item because any repairs will inevitably involve reweaving.

Most basketwoven pieces are made of thin under-and-over lacings which connect, position and support the basic framework of thicker twigs.

These thin bindings are not too difficult to replace, but the thicker 'ribs' are extremely difficult — if not impossible — to replace. Avoid taking on any furniture with these 'ribs' smashed or split.

Tough and aged bindings will probably demand cutting tools much stronger than scissors. Plier-type snips or garden pruners are both good. New bindings are soaked in water to make them supple before they are laced in.

Painting and varnishing
Brushing paint on to any kind of woven or bound structure is quite a laborious process and for such items spray painting is by far the best technique to use.

A decent aerosol will contain as much as 400 grammes (about 14 ounces) of paint, enough to cover a good-sized chair twice over. The golden rule for all spray painting is to put on thin coats, and allow plenty of drying time in between, until you produce the required finish.

62 Below: The natural cane chairs add a friendly touch to this bedroom setting. Notice the cleverly arranged frames for displaying favourite pictures.

EASY RE-UPHOLSTERY FOR CHAIR SEATS

The development of foam and other modern materials has made upholstery much easier for the amateur, although time and patience are still essential.

Foam padding principles

Begin with an absolutely firm foundation for the tacks, filling in old tack-holes with slivers of hardwood rather than knife-in fillers. Err (if at all) on the generous side when deciding how many webbing strands to put in: it's the easiest job of all, and all the work you do after is wasted if the foundation sags. Smooth off any roughness wherever covers are to be stretched over edges.

Above all, pull down foam edges evenly. A pair of upholsterer's pliers helps enormously with this: they have square-looking, flat jaws which grip a fair width very firmly. Of course, you do not have to pull at the foam itself. Instead, this must always have un-bleached calico strips stuck to the edges whenever pulling or stretching is necessary. More details are given below.

Pincushion padding

This method of upholstering a seat produces the neatest appearance when it is used on a previously cane-bottomed chair, which will have a shallow rebate around the edge. The bottom of such a chair may or may not still be sound enough to hold tacks. If it is, the webbing is tacked down into it, stopping about $\frac{1}{4}$ inch (6mm.) short of the rebate side to allow room for the anchorage of the foam pad and the cover.

Cut 1-inch (25mm.) foam to the shape of the rebate, but $\frac{1}{4}$ inch smaller all around. Then trim its edges with scissors so that they are bevelled at an angle less than 45°. Now stick calico strips to the foam edges, 2 inches wide (51mm.) and two to a side. These are used together to pull and to hold the foam in place so that the bevel is forced down to make a gently curved finish.

Before you tack the foam down, stick fill-in pieces of webbing into the spaces which separate the support strips. This will help to prevent un-sightly ripples. Drive in the tacks very precisely along the line where foam edge meets chair. This is hard to do but vital, (a one-handed punch helps).

Having cut off all the spare calico, you can fit the cover. The nailing sequence when doing this is very

important. Be sure to fit all tacks loosely into position before driving any of them home.

First spike the middle of each side, then the front edge, working out from the centre to within an inch or two of each corner. The back row is next, then each side in turn. Cut back the cover-piece to project to a reasonable hem-width beginning from the tack lines. This hem may be almost negligible if the material is thick, but it is still better to turn it under. Do this by lifting out all the tacks, a side at a time, and putting them in again (for the last time) after turning the hem under. Do not forget to snip away excess thickness at the corners.

Damaged chair bottoms

Where a rebate is too lacerated to take more tacks, tack the webbing up to the underside of the chair frame and fill in the extra depth with additional foam. In very bad cases you may then have to anchor the remaining upholstery to the wooden strip outside the rebate.

63 Opposite: This simple wooden chair has been turned into an impressive feature for any room, with a few coats of paint and a simple-to-make seat cover and cushion in a dramatic floral print.

Drop-in chair seats

1. With the cut edge of the webbing facing in, tack it down with 3 tacks in a triangle. Turn the webbing over and tack again with 3 tacks in a reverse triangle.
2. Stretch the webbing across to the front of the frame using a strainer.
3. Tack the webbing again with 3 tacks. Leave an inch spare after cutting and turn this back over the first tacks. Fix with 3 tacks in a reverse triangle. Do the same for each piece.
4. Copy the webbing pattern on the original upholstery where possible.
5. Cover the webbing with hessian, tacking it to the frame ½ inch from the edge of the fabric. Tack these raw edges down.
6. Place tape at each edge of the foam as shown.
7. Place the foam on the hessian and tack the free edge of the tape to the frame. As the foam is larger than the frame it will form a dome.
8. For the cover: make a double pleat at the corners and tack the centre point. Fold the excess fabric into pleats and tack. Cut off excess fabric and cover the seat bottom with a piece of linen. Fold under all raw edges and tack.

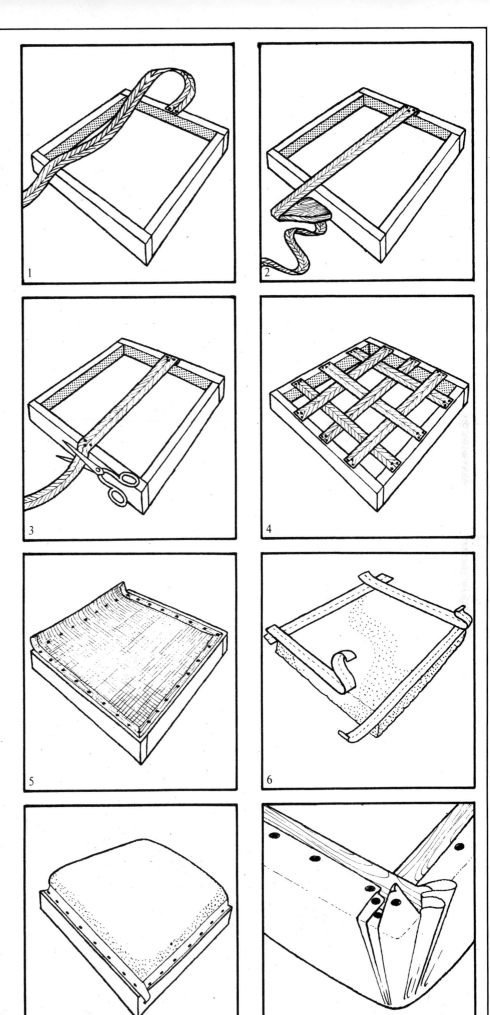

SPRUNG UPHOLSTERY

Button Chesterfields are still one of the most elegant furniture styles, and beautifully finished ones are usually quite expensive. It is possible, however, to buy a shabby old Chesterfield (not necessarily buttoned) at a low price and to re-cover it for a fraction of the cost you would pay for a new one.

A few precautions

While a complete novice should not begin upholstering on a button Chesterfield it is perfectly feasible for someone with a bit of experience to attempt. Competence in buttoning and pleating is important—and patience is particularly necessary. This project may take you over a month to complete, but do not rush or try to invent any short cuts. The techniques given here are applicable to all seating that is sprung and filled.

Stripping down

Strip the sofa down to the bare wood frame, removing every tack and scrap of fabric. Fill in any holes with plastic wood and rub them down with abrasive paper once the filler has dried. Make any other repairs to joints, etc, and treat the frame for woodworm if necessary. (Do this last so as not to affect any adhesive you may need to use.) After treating for woodworm, allow the frame to dry for at least a week.

Back and side fillings

Follow the step-by-steps for lashing the springs and filling the seat with the coconut fibre. Do the same for the back and arms, and cover with the light canvas. Tack the canvas in place along all edges except the arm fronts. At this point the fabric is stitched as shown in the drawings and the filling is tied to the 'sandwich' canvases.

Button preparation

Mark out the planned positions of the buttons on the light canvas. With the scissors cut a diagonal 1½-inch (35mm.) slit where each button will be placed. Open out the filling by clearing a 'shaft' 1¼ inches in diameter through each slit. Do this by inserting the flat end of the regulator through the slit and forcing the filling away from the slit all the way down to the base canvas. This will allow the buttons to sink deeply.

The top cover patterns

Ten pieces of fabric are needed for the cover – a front border panel, seat, inside and outside back, two inside

arms, two outside arms and two facing panels for the arms. To work out the dimensions of each piece, measure the length and width of each of the above areas, then add 4 inches (100mm) to each measurement to account for the filling and buttoning. Transfer the final dimensions to a sheet of cheap muslin and cut out. These pieces are placed over the final filling to check that the pattern fits, and are then used to outline the cutting for the final covers.

The final covering

Once you have cut out the final cover you can proceed to stitch it in place. The seat cover is lockstitched along the front edge, stretched over the filling, compressing the horsehair to 1 inch (25mm), and tacked in place along the back and sides. The back, arms, and front panel are done in the same way, but with these panels the buttons must be placed and secured and the material pleated before the fabric is tacked down. The arms are pleated in 'rays' before tacking down. Stitch and tack all remaining covers in place.

Buttoning

To place the buttons, thread a needle and push the eye of it (an upholstery needle is pointed at both ends) through the outside cover and through the shaft in the coconut fibre. When

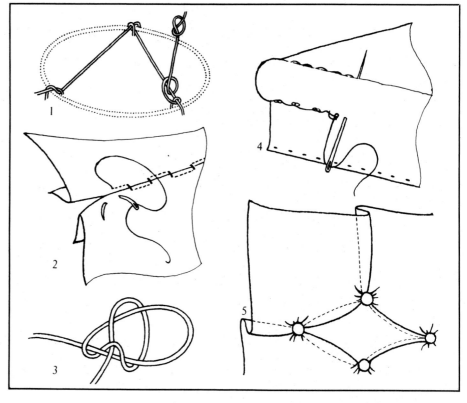

64 Opposite: With care and patience you can transform a dowdy, old-fashioned sofa into an elegant, fashionable button-back.
Above: 1. Method for securing the springs to the webbing, and the canvas to the tops of the springs.
2. A slip-stitch, used to fasten the light canvas over back and side fillings.
3. A slip-knot, used for pulling the buttons down.
4. The front edge of the seat being stitched in a roll.
5. A pleating detail.

the eye of the needle has just pierced the base canvas, place a 1-inch scrap of webbing between the twine and the needle. This will act as an anchor and prevent the twins from pulling through the canvas.

Pull the other end of the needle back through the canvas, cut through the main cover, and secure the twine tight so that the slip knot forces the button into the filling. Leave the ends loose with about a 4-inch (100mm.) loose end. When all buttons are fitted, knot each length of twine, cut the loose ends to ½ inch and tuck under the button (see diagrams).

As each button is sunk into position, the fabric is pleated out to take up the excess material. The front panel is pleated vertically, and the back and side ones are diamond pleated.

Essential tools and materials:
Tools you will need are: a mallet with a 100mm or 4 inch head, a ripping chisel for removing tacks, a 6 ounce claw or Warrington hammer, a webbing stretcher, heavy duty scissors (230mm or 9 inches), a curved spring needle, a heavy straight needle (250mm or 10 inches long) for the main stitching, a light straight needle (250mm) for buttoning, a small curved needle (75mm or 3 inches) for finishing edge joints.
Materials you will need are (quantities vary with the size of the unit): webbing to anchor the springs at the base, springs, heavy canvas (about 12 ounces), light canvas or scrim (about 7½ ounces), coconut fibre for the first stuffing, horsehair for the 'top' filling, upholstery wadding, upholstery tacks, 3-ply sisal cord for lashing the springs, flax twine for stitching and buttoning, cover fabric and a quantity of buttons pre-covered in matching fabric.

1. With the frame upside down secure the webbing across the bottom rails. Begin with strips running from back to front. After tacking each strip at the rear, use the stretcher to pull the webbing across the frame and hold it while 4 securing nails are driven in.

2. When the webbing has been stretched across the frame in a basketweave pattern, the frame is turned right side up and the springs are stitched down with the curved spring needle.

3. The springs are compressed about 35mm (1½ inches) and kept in place by knotting sisal along the tops and securing at the outer edges of the frame.

4. When the seat springs have been compressed and tied, heavy canvas is laid over and nailed to the frame rails. Work from back to front to sides. Then stitch the canvas to the tops of the springs as shown on the previous page.

5. The positioning for the arm and back springs: the lashing is only carried out horizontally.

6. Lay 102mm (4 inches) of coconut fibre over the seat and cover with light canvas so the fibre is compressed about 35mm.

7. Tack the light canvas along the back and side rails and stitch it along the front as shown on the previous page. Then anchor the filling between the two canvases as shown.

8. Cut diagonal slits for the buttons and clear the fibre stuffing down to the base canvas.

9. Horsehair stuffing is placed over the second seat canvas. Anchor strands of twine to the canvas and pull them up through the stuffing.

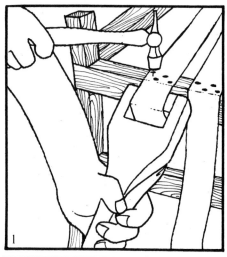

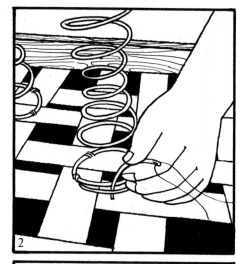

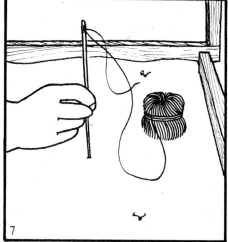

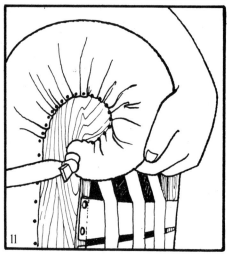

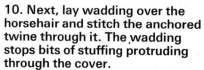

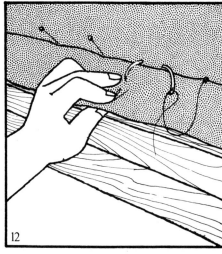

10. Next, lay wadding over the horsehair and stitch the anchored twine through it. The wadding stops bits of stuffing protruding through the cover.

11. This shows the pleating and fitting procedure for the front of the arms. Pay particular attention to this point – it acts as a mould for the final cover.

12. Laying the final canvas over the seat. Skewers or pins hold the material in place while it is being stitched.

13. Pulling the button through. The line at the opposite end is anchored to the base canvas by a scrap roll of webbing.

14. Pleating and buttoning. These are done together to accommodate the quantity of loose material.

15. Pleating the final cover around the front edges of the arm rest. The nails in the middle are covered with a separate panel of material.

16. Running the skirting panel along the front. When stitched, the material is pleated down and nailed under the rail.

17. Fitting the top seat panel. This is stitched along the front, pleated over to the back and nailed along the back.

18. Stitching the arm cover panel in place.

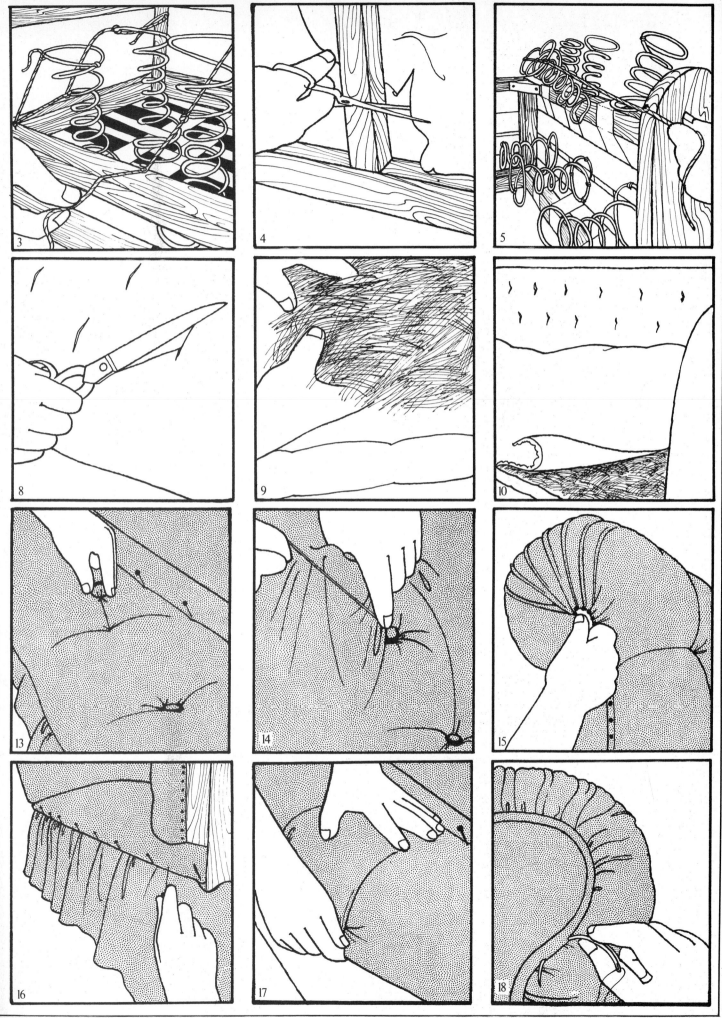

THE LOOK OF LEATHER

Real leather in new condition is almost impossible to distinguish from man-made imitations, some of which are good enough to deceive experts, if only outside their laboratories.

The older it gets, however, the more its advantages over the plastics become apparent, if it's been looked after. If it hasn't, the more its short-comings will become evident.

Features to look for

As it grew originally on an animal, a hide naturally has a grain (running from nose to tail) and pores (all over). Invariably it is smoother on the out-side than on the inside. Different animals produce different grades of leather, as do older or younger beasts of the same kind, and so do different parts of the same hide.

Unless hide is tanned to convert it into leather, it simply rots away — something it can still do eventually if its surface is allowed to crack and its softer layers to absorb water. In this condition, leather is prey to moulds and fungi which cause its layers to separate.

This separation is what to look for in secondhand leather-covered furni-ture. If it's disintegrating, don't imagine there's anything you can do to save it. Even in the sorriest state, it may cost you heavily to buy it, and a total re-covering job will dwarf that expenditure.

Cosmetic colour

Damage to the leather surface caused by cutting, tearing or burning may be quite extensive, but not enough to affect the overall soundness of a piece. In these circumstances, any one of a number of proprietary paints, polishes or colouring compounds can very effectively restore its respectability. Popular motoring magazine advertise-ments are a good source for renova-ting paints, and women's magazines for shoe-colourings. Neither will do its best for you if the leather is very greasy, so wipe it over with methylated spirit on a rag before you start.

Feeding and maintenance

Upholsterers and leather-goods shops usually stock a thick white cream called 'Hide Food'. This should be used regularly for cleaning and polish-ing leather furniture, once you have it in reasonable condition. Good advice normally offered on the jar is 'little and often'. Take it.

Opposite: The before and after looks of leather-covered furniture: for large recovering jobs, some of the man-made vinyls will provide superb results – and at an economical price.

Patching a tear

A split will very probably have appeared along the grain of the leather, as a result of some sharp object or corner penetrating a panel. Catch it soon after it has been done and the problem is less because there isn't likely to be any loss of leather, or panel deformation. A small patch should, then, do the trick.

Short tears and long tears

Short tears are far easier to patch, since the panel they appear in isn't likely to have lost tension and you will still have a fairly firm ground to apply your patch to. With a longer rip you may have the twin problems of floppy edges and lack of easy access behind to enable you to bring the torn edges together, even temporarily, without recourse to stitching. Unless you can release one or two sides of the panel to secure the loose edges from the back, you may have to loop them together with twine.

Considerable strength may be demanded of a patch if it is to hold a long tear securely, so allow a generous area for the adhesive to get a grip on either side of the tear and at each end. A patch's permanence will depend on the area covered, on the strength of the bond and on the character of the adhesive. Strongest of all are the epoxy resin types, now on the market in quick-setting forms, which make *ad hoc* jobs like leather patching possible.

Although the bond given by epoxies is extremely strong, it is not flexible, so on panels which are liable to flexing strains it might be better to use a less durable but more flexible contact adhesive. Almost any will be suitable for leather-to-leather joins.

No matter what the adhesive you use, in any situation, and no matter what surfaces you are joining, failure of the bond is almost a certainty unless you thoroughly de-grease the areas. Leather is more likely than most materials to hold traces of grease, oil or wax, so take a little extra trouble to make sure of removing all traces.

Smooth edges for patches

When you buy a bicycle puncture repair kit, you will usually find that the patches are chamfered off to a feather edge, so that they will not catch on the outer tyre as you reinstall the tube. When patching leather furniture, you will need to make your own patches, which will not, obviously, have this facility. As all good bookbinders know, it is possible to plane leather down from the suede side until it is so thin you can almost read through it. Some do this by scraping with a convex knife blade, some with a sharp spoke-shave or modelling knife, some with a low-angle block plane. Spokeshaves and planes should have the cutter honed to a slight curve, and the mouth set fairly wide, to achieve the best results.

Leather-topped desk repairs

Faced with the prospect of having to replace the leather facing of a desk top, first decide whether or not you can really afford to use leather. A desk top panel is usually quite large, so that the supplier will probably have to charge you for the whole hide, not just a portion.

Consider, instead, a plastic imitation which has much to recommend it for this purpose. It is tough, easy to keep clean, needs no feeding, comes in a great variety of colours and patterns and will not rot. Extreme cold is perhaps its worst enemy, but a desk is not likely to encounter that.

Truly old but inexpensive desks will have simply had the original leather fixed to the top like a postage stamp with strips of veneer placed around the edges to finish off. This type is the easiest to renovate. You just scrape away the old covering scraps, thoroughly clean the bottom of the shallow tray beneath the covering, refinish the veneer and put in the new covering.

Paper templates are useful for determining the exact shape of the new panel. Once cut, it should be fitted dry, since the edges must meet the veneer accurately. If you attempt this with adhesive about, you will find that the edges are very hard to snip cleanly. A contact adhesive with a bit of slip, such as the thixotropic Dunlop Thixofix, can be used for this job. You may find, however, that you have more opportunity for adjustment if you use a PVA woodwork adhesive, spread over the top with a brush. Then you can unroll and position the vinyl covering and set the glue by means of a cool iron.

Any glue squeezed out at the edges should be wiped away with a damp rag immediately, before it sets.

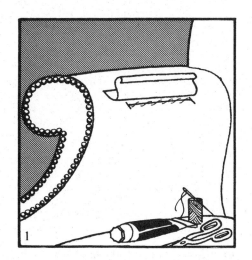

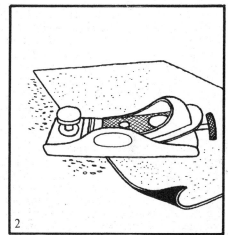

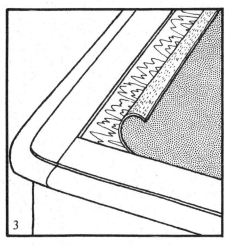

1. Patching a long tear in a leather piece will need some stitching to provide a firm ground for the patch.
2. Block plain the edges of a leather patch so that they will not catch on things.

3. On a desk top, roll out the vinyl covering over a PVA woodwork adhesive.
4. Position the covering and set the glue by pressing down with a very cool iron.

WISE BUYS

Older secondhand office furniture and ancillary equipment represent some of the best value for money in terms of residual life and sheer utility. Three main sources of supply are open to you: dealers, auctions and the private sales advertised in newspapers.

Sources of secondhand office furniture

Dealers in used office furniture may be specialists in secondhand items or they may be in business chiefly as office furnishers, who must take in items as part exchange for any new equipment which they sell. If the latter is the case, they are likely to be satisfied with lower prices than the specialists, since they make their main profit on selling new items.

Many auction sales are arranged by a legal official in charge of bankruptcy proceedings. This official arranges to sell off a business's assets to pay the debts. Much of this furniture is sold long before it has had the normal amount of wear, so it is particularly good value.

Sales of used office furniture advertised primarily through newspapers are also likely to concern little-used items. If, however, the advertiser is also the firm which has been using the furniture, the quality is probably reflected in the price.

Doorstep sales

If you work in an office you may have the chance, when any of the furniture is traded in for new, to buy the occasional piece at an exceptionally favourable price. Usually the dealer or supplier will make a list of the trade-ins, noting what he is allowing the firm against each one. Since it makes no difference to him or to the firm who actually buys any of the items, it is often possible to get what you want at the notional figure — the only difficulty being that you may have to remove it at your own expense at very short notice.

The spoils of vigilance

The bigger the collection of office furniture you can find to search among, the more numerous and pleasant your trophies can be. Force your imagination beyond the hatstands or waste-paper baskets, even beyond tables and chairs. Take your chances with different, often overlooked items and you may find some exciting bargains.

What you may find

Although the great majority of furniture available falls into the table and chair category, an enormous variety of equipment can be the reward of a more persistent search. Trolleys with shelves are not uncommon, and you will find cabinets for books, files or drawings. The latter are very useful, having wide and shallow drawers.

Working wonders with wood

Ancient wooden pieces will most likely be sturdily built from solid wood (usually oak), internally filthy, externally battered and drearily finished. If, however, the timber is solid and relatively unwarped, you have a real find, appearances being deceptive. A good clean, complete strip and refinish will soon transform the surface, especially if you go to a little trouble to find some handsome hardware like ornamental handles.

Wooden tops and shelves can be re-faced with plastic laminate if they are too badly damaged for renovation, or if you want to use them for heat-resistant purposes.

Metamorphosis in metal

Apparently unprepossessing metal furniture may very well be worth a second look. Try to see it free from the ugly cloak of its drab, institutional grey or green paint and think only of its utility value. Structural deterioration is not encountered nearly as often in metal constructions as it is in wooden ones. Much of the battering such pieces receive damages only the paintwork, which is easily replaced.

In fact, you can usually assume that surface defects can be repaired invisibly with no great trouble. However, you should avoid items with moving parts that have ceased to operate properly, unless, of course, you are convinced that the only thing needed to put them right is a drop of oil.

Generally office furniture is mass-produced without any thought as to how it can be mended. One very good reason for this is that the cost of repairs can be almost as much as that of replacing it. Hinges, for example, are probably brazed on instead of being fastened with nuts and bolts.

Dents in sheet metal are fairly easy to deal with, unless they have deformed a door or drawer so that it will not shut properly. Small dents can be knocked out against a piece of blockboard, but use a plastic-faced hammer to avoid making a further dent in the process.

Many deeper dents, scratches or holes respond to the same treatment you might give the dents in your car: glass fibre matting, resin filler and/or cellulose putty.

Repainting

A few of the items you may come across will probably have been stove-enamelled, but most will have been given a factory coating of cellulose lacquer, assisted to dry with a bit of heat. Whatever paint is left on the metal will have very good adhesion, and will be thin enough to allow bare patches to be covered without the edges showing through.

Steel wool. soap pads are effective to use in cleaning and smoothing the surface for repainting. Rinse the area well with clean water after using the pads and wipe over with methylated spirit or a mineral turpentine substitute when dry.

100 per cent polyurethane paints have the best properties for painting metal. (The 100 per cent refers to what is left on the surface when the film is dry: about 30 per cent of what you can buy consists of driers and solvents which help in the application.) If you are accustomed to using ordinary alkyd paints, which respond to being drawn out fairly thin, you have probably developed a technique that is unhelpful when it comes to working with polyurethane paints. They do not appreciate being pulled about, so be sure to study the manufacturer's recommended technique. Load the brush reasonably well, empty it in one grand gesture, lightly spread the pool of paint as far as it will easily and quickly go, then brush off with featherlight strokes. Leaving it alone at this stage may be the hardest part, but success may depend on it so do not be tempted to dab at small patches.

If you have trouble in maintaining a wet edge, remember that you can thin down pure polyurethane paints far more than you can alkyds, without affecting their toughness. A mineral turpentine substitute or heating paraffin are safe diluents. Polyurethanes take a week to reach full hardness. It is especially important on metals to allow the whole drying period.

Stick on finishes

Fabrics, wallpapers, upholstery plastics, PVC vinyl coverings can all be used to soften the harshness of metal panels. In addition, should the resonance of perhaps a cupboard top become annoying, there are self-adhesive sound-deadening pads, such as those made by Bostik for cars, which you can fix underneath.

66 Opposite: Office furniture is so plentiful and usually so reasonably priced that it makes good sense to use it in the home. Metal file cabinets, or office cupboards — cleaned out, painted and lined, if necessary, can do good service as containers for clothes or linen. A small desk can be the answer to your need for a dressing table, and chairs or stools, painted cheerful shiny colours are welcome anywhere.

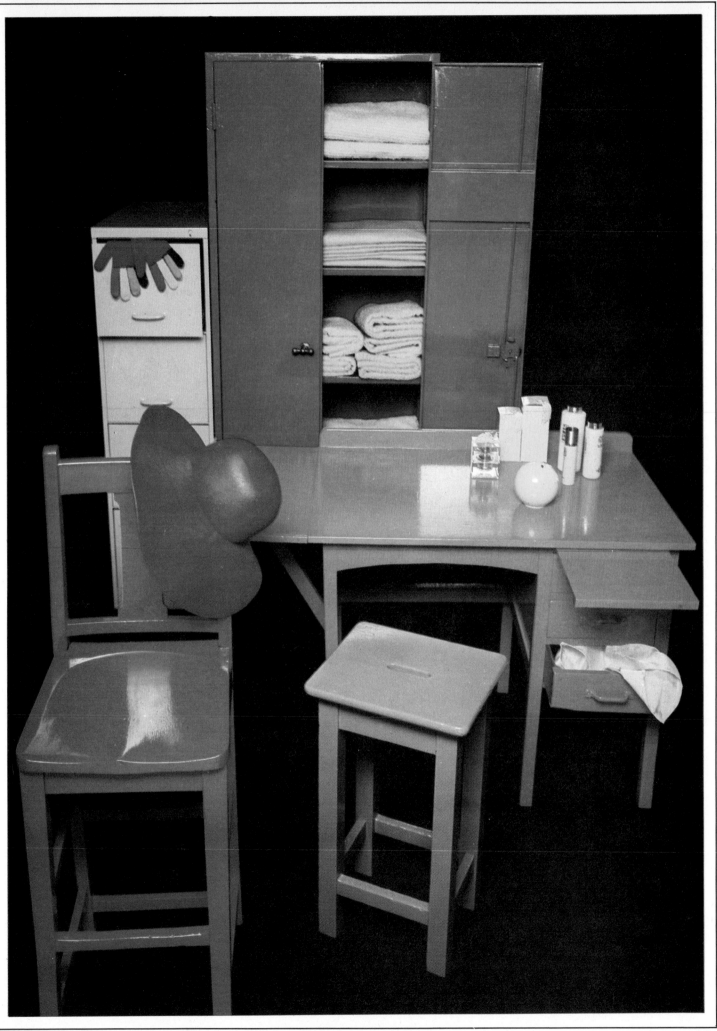

TIN, IRON AND MARBLE

Coffee pots, hot-water jugs and similar utensils used to be made from an alloy called Britannia metal, almost entirely tin with a small percentage of antimony. It had a very pleasing, silvery colour which lost little of its brightness with use or time. Unfortunately, if you happened to forget that it was made chiefly of tin and placed it over a gas ring to keep it warm, its very low melting point immediately became apparent!

Apart from this drawback, Britannia metal was extremely serviceable, primarily because tin resists tarnishing and most common forms of chemical attack. It is this property which has made it the natural choice for protective coatings on less resistant metals, such as steel.

Tinplate is composed of very thin sheet steel which is coated on both sides by a hot-dip process with an even thinner layer of tin. The object is to combine the strength of steel with the chemically inert, softer tin. The result works beautifully – until the tin coating is pierced, from which point onwards the steel underneath begins to rust. Sometimes this happens because the tin is accidentally knocked or scratched, sometimes because it has worn thin through dust, abrasion or other storage maltreatment. In this case many rust spots can start simultaneously, giving the appearance that the tin itself is going rusty.

De-rusting techniques
The method you use to eliminate rust on a tinplate article will depend on how you intend to finish it afterwards. Generally speaking, one of the rust-removing types of paint, which turn the rust into something else, is preferable from the permanent point of view. A wash-off, rust-eating jelly may, however, be a good idea if you intend clear-sealing, especially if the rust patches are above pinhole-size. Power wire-brushing would probably do more harm than good on such thin metal.

Painting tinplate
One popular use for tinplate used to be to make hearth plates. These were used to protect the floor immediately in front of an open-fronted cooking range from hot falling cinders. If you do find one of these and intend using it in such a situation, first find your-self a heat-resistant, non-flammable paint. Originally, the plate will probably have been vitreous-enamelled.

DIY Repairs
Sheet metalwork is a skilled trade, and one that requires a great deal of expensive equipment. Unless you have exceptional knowledge, a comprehensive tool kit and a well-equipped workshop, ambitious re-forming jobs on tinplate will be difficult to carry out successfully.

Drilling and crease-flattening should be done with a piece of flat wood held under the sheet to prevent unintentional denting. Fabricated-panel constructions are best repaired with the aid of a modern pop-riveting gun, which uses hollow rivets. Once the rivet is in place, threaded through the prepared holes, the gun draws a special nail through it which turns its edges over to hold the sheets together.

Twisted hinges on tinplate boxes are especially difficult to mend. Look carefully before you buy. Do not worry about missing keys on tin-trunk locks, though. Just be glad you have been lucky enough to find a tin trunk. If you can remove the lock easily, take it to a locksmith, who can then make a new key. If you cannot get it off, try taking the whole trunk to the locksmith.

Decorating tinplate
Tinplate was often black japanned, but unless you particularly want to do a purist's renovation job, a modern 100 per cent polyurethane finish has perhaps the best combination of hardness and flexibility to cope with tinplate's tendency to flex and crease.

Self-adhesive vinyl materials can be used to good effect on tin, both internally and externally. Some felt-like nylon flock variations now on the market are especially useful for sticking to the bottoms of boxes or trays to protect table tops from scratches. The material is cut, peeled from its backing and fixed in exactly the same way as ordinary vinyl coverings, such as Fablon. Such materials could also be used to line tinplate carry-alls, dispatch-boxes and cash-boxes.

Iron age furniture and fittings
Of the many different forms which iron appears in, the two most common in the furnishing field are cast iron and wrought iron.

As a rule, an object made of cast iron indicates that the material has been cast straight from a little blast-furnace called a cupola. Hardly any measures are taken to remove impurities in the process. The iron resulting is rather coarse, needing to be cast into fairly massive forms to ensure adequate strength.

Park benches, manhole covers, garden seats and tables, street lamps and fireplaces all bear testimony to the lack of tensile strength in the metal.

Sheer mass can, however, be an advantage from the point of view of withstanding the ravages of time. Cast iron may rust, but there is plenty of it for the rust to nibble at, and even quite badly rusted pieces are well worth salvaging.

Really thick rust is unlikely to be found on fireplaces. But if you embark on de-rusting a heavily encrusted garden seat or table which constantly lives with its feet in moist ground, remember that rust can creep under any paint or lacquer you care to put on, once it is given a start. Try every means in your power to lay the object on its back so that you can get the rust off the feet. Remove rust as you would from tinplate; the only difference being that power wire-brushing may be used, especially on heavily encrusted surfaces.

Wrought iron
Any wrought iron work you find outside expensive salesrooms is more than likely done in mild steel, since the word 'wrought' now refers to the method involved in making the metal and not the metal itself.

Manufacturing wrought iron is an ancient and honourable trade, the process for refining it having been brought to perfection in the 1780s. It is an elastic metal, with a stringy, tough structure. Once it had been through the refining process it was removed from the furnaces in great blobs wound on to the ends of poles. In the process the metal never reached the molten state, so the iron already had a well-defined texture when it reached the rolling mills. By the time they had pummelled it into bars, it was the most ductile ferrous metal on the market. It was widely used wherever good nature and strength were needed – until mild steel replaced it.

Mild steel has been around for a considerable time, so if you do come across genuine wrought iron you will have quite a find. File some and see. Wrought iron files easily, but blocks the file very quickly, making it unusable after a few strokes. Neither mild steel nor cast iron have so severe an effect.

De-rusting and painting techniques are the same as those for cast iron. Much wrought iron work, however, has angles where strips are riveted or brazed together and where rust can linger if you do not take extra trouble to reach it with whatever chemical you have decided to use.

Re-using marble slabs
In the days before plastic laminates, marble was widely used for table tops – especially those used for preparing food. It was, nevertheless, always relatively expensive and appeared mainly on large scale furniture appropriate to the spacious dwellings of those people who could afford it.

A good, thick, marble top will outlast several table underframes, so you may be lucky enough to find a slab reasonably priced, in terms of cash per square metre. However, if it is very large you may have the problem of fitting it into a small place. Because it looks like hard, coloured glass, marble does tend to give the impression of being totally unyielding and indivisible, but in fact it is not very difficult to cut.

Like glass, marble is crystalline in structure, but there the similarity ends. It is far softer. A masonry-cutting disc mounted in the circular saw attachment of a handyman's power drill will cut through it, but not much faster than you could do by hand.

First of all, the slab must be scored and broken in much the same way as you would a ceramic tile, but there are important differences. Draw a clear line with a soft pencil where the division is to be, and then continue it round all four faces: top, bottom and both front and back edges. Notch the two edges deeply with a hacksaw. You need go in only to the depth of the blade, which will be worn out by the time you finish the second notch.

Score deeply along the line on both sides, with a carbide-tipped tile-cutting tool. Then support the slab on either side of the line (a fair distance from it) and stand on it. It should only be a few inches from ground level. The result should be a clean break.

Polishing the raw edges is done with a grinding brick, a milled file or a special type of toothed plane, such as Surform, with the 508 pattern heavy-duty blade in it. To finish off, rub down with wet-and-dry abrasive paper used wet, in combination with any fine cutting compounds or polishing rouge. Remember not to leave sharp corners.

67 Top: Wrought or cast iron furniture need not be confined to a garden. This spacious-looking dining room has a light, out-door atmosphere which has been enhanced by using white cast iron chairs, plant stands and a cathedral stove for the main furnishings. The stove could be fitted with a light if it's no longer used for heating. Your local garage may be willing to sandblast items which are encrusted with paint and rust.
Above left: Tin fish moulds keep their shiny glow with a coat of clear polyurethane finish.
Above right: Marble slabs were once used widely for table tops and washstands but today they're a bit more unusual. It's one way of giving an ordinary chest or table a special look.

RESTORING THE GLOW TO BRASS AND COPPER

Too plentiful to be classed as a precious metal, copper has always had a high place in mankind's esteem because of its many useful properties. Perhaps more than any other metal, it is used widely in practically pure form. At its purest, it is almost as good as silver as a conductor of heat and electricity.

Pleasant in colour and easy to handle, copper is highly resistant to weather and salt water corrosion. It will, however, over a long period of time, form a green 'rust' on its surface. This coating can be quite attractive on some things, such as building domes, and the initial thin layer seems to protect the underlying metal. Household items that you may come across made from relatively pure copper will be those which require good heat conductivity such as kettles, saucepans, frying pans and warming pans.

A sociable metal
Copper very readily forms alloys with other metals, but in the secondhand field the two most frequently encountered are brass and bronze.

The brass group
Copper + zinc = brass is a very simple equation for this metal. Generally, alloys containing more than 80 per cent copper are used as gilding metals. Their richer colouring makes them especially useful for making things like costume jewellery. The ordinary articles you might encounter, such as paraffin lamps, doorknobs and candlesticks, are more likely to be made in Muntz metal — roughly 60 per cent copper to 40 per cent zinc.

The bronzes
Copper and tin alloyed together make bronze. You are most likely to encounter gunmetal bronzes, which have a bit less copper in them than coinage-alloy types, a little more tin and odd scraps of zinc, lead and/or nickel.

Spit and polish
Neither brass nor bronze is liable to quite such severe discoloration as neglected copper. Normally it responds very well to ordinary metal polishes. These usually consist of a weak acid and a selection of abrasives, perhaps with a little wax to help the shine along.

Copper cooking utensils may give you some cleaning problems, due to contact with heat and fumes. Those in the picture, for example, were almost totally black when they were bought. Vinegar with plenty of salt boiled up in it was used to clean them, helped by a bit of scouring powder. The mixture was rubbed onto the pots with a nylon scouring pad until brightness returned to the metal. As soon as this stage was reached, the pans were rinsed and dried. Had they been left wet, the dark copper oxide would have formed again.

Mending leaks
Holes in copper or brass utensils may be the result of general wear, particularly if an item has been used for cooking and so been subjected to repeated scouring. If the metal has worn paper-thin, its cooking days are over, but it may still have a decorative role to play. In this event, you need only disguise the hole by filling it up with car-body resin filler. This can then be dabbed with metallic copper-coloured lacquer, such as that made by Rustins.

Repairs for active service
If a hole has been accidentally made in still serviceably thick and sound metal, or if a metal seam is leaking, such as around a kettle's spout, or along a seam in a paraffin lamp's reservoir, a soldered repair is the best and most permanent solution.

Solder is produced by amalgamating lead with tin or other metals to make a compound which will melt easily, flow into any cranny and bond instantly to the metal. By altering the proportions of the different ingredients, the solder's melting point can be predetermined. You can always find a grade which will melt before your copper or brass utensil does (very important) but which will not melt again at cooking temperatures (equally important). It helps if you can explain

68 Left: A collection of copper pots makes a handsome surround for a kitchen fireplace — or can look equally well hanging against a wall.
Above: The rich look of brass is used for all sorts of easy-to-find household items — from bed frames and lamps to door knobs. Don't be put off if some old brass pieces are coated with a brown, shoe-polish like substance: a hard scrub with a metal polish should restore their looks.

what you want to use the solder for when you buy it.

Solder will not bond firmly unless the metal is completely free from oxides, a condition difficult to obtain, since oxidation is speeded up when a metal is heated. Strips of solder with a core of flux will solve this problem. The flux either seals the metal off from the air to stop oxides from forming or it removes the oxides chemically, according to whether it is an active or a passive kind of flux.

Chemical colour changing

Corroded brass or copper might look uncomfortably brash and new after the scouring you have been obliged to give for cleaning. Provided that you have a decently polished surface on the metal, you can treat it with chemicals to alter its colour to some degree. You must always take the obvious precautions against skin or eye contact and against spillage, but the results

can be well worth a little extra trouble.

One of the simplest mixtures to use is a weak solution of ammonium sulphide. A good soaking in this will give brass a golden hue, or copper a reddish one. The strength of the solution can be varied quite a bit — a stronger solution and/or longer soaking will produce various shades of black, brown, red or yellow. Always rinse the metal after using this solution, and finish off with a coat of lacquer. Polyurethane or melamine clear lacquers are probably the most suitable for decorative purposes.

Antiquing brass and copper

To give brass a green/brown colour, make up a solution of copper nitrate in water by adding 100 grammes of copper nitrate to 100 millilitres of water, with larger or smaller amounts pro rata. Do not add the water to the chemical. (This is a good general rule

to follow when dealing with all chemicals: the reason being that the heat generated could vaporize water droplets which could then spit in your eye.) Heat the solution to a temperature of 60°C (140°F) and brush it all over the metal every few hours throughout a day. Leave the article overnight.

Dry it off by placing the item in a warm oven for a little while, then rub French chalk over it with a soft brush. Finally remove any traces of the chalk with a dry rag, and lacquer over.

It is possible to 'silver' brass, for a clock face, perhaps. To do this use a paste consisting of 10 grammes of silver chloride, 20 grammes of cream of tartar and 30 grammes of common salt. Grind all the ingredients up and mix with just enough water to make it into a paste the consistency of cream. Rub the paste over the brass with a soft rag until you have the degree of silvering you want, then wash off the excess, dry and lacquer.

SILVER AND CHROME

Chromium is an extremely hard metal, and a rather expensive one, so solid chromium items are virtually non-existent. It appears mainly as a thin, electro-plated film on literally thousands of common, everyday things made from cheaper materials.

The character of chromium
Most of the problems with chromium plating arise when it is applied to iron or steel. Although hard, the film of chromium is porous, allowing moisture through to whatever is immediately beneath it. Good chromium plating consists of a thin coat of copper to give good adhesion to the basic metal, a fat layer of nickel (which is non-porous) over this and a final film of chromium.

Items such as bathroom fittings are usually made of brass, and receive a specially heavy coat of nickel, but those made of iron or steel do not, and should be watched carefully for signs of rust. Minute black pits are the first hint that water has penetrated to corrodible metal. Leave the pitted chrome untreated and the rust will creep along the ferrous metal's surface to undermine the plating completely, so that it just flakes away.

Protecting sound chrome
Unpitted plating can be protected quite adequately by frequent applications of one of the heavier wax polishes which have been specially made for the chrome parts of motor vehicles. Make certain, however, that the polish claims to seal out moisture for lengthy periods, not just to clean.

Treating pitted chrome
Waxes will only succeed if you seal off the pores in the chromium before any moisture has penetrated to start rust spots. Once pitted, you must deal with the rust, however minute in quantity. Any proprietary rust remover will do some good, but for this particular problem you should choose one, such as Kurust, that does not have to be washed off with water. These change the rust chemically into a non-corroding compound and are the most likely to work.

These rust removers are especially effective in stopping rust under chrome, but often introduce other problems. Some varieties refuse to dry soundly over the good plating. When this happens, the chrome will neither shine nor support lacquer properly, unless you follow up with a specially made companion wash to remove the surplus, chemically-unchanged compound. Once this has been done, a glossy, transparent polyurethane lacquer will seal off the treated surface completely, long-lastingly and almost invisibly.

Badly rusted plating
Provided that there is no extensive flaking or lifting of the plating film, even quite severely rusted chrome plate can be rescued for a time if you precede the remover/wash/lacquer treatment with a steel wool scrub. Domestic soap pads will do, if you rinse well enough and dry off all the water before you put the remover on. The lacquer will effectively disguise much of the unavoidable fine scratching made by the steel wool. Maintenance should not involve more than the occasional clean, (not polish), and new application of lacquer.

Chromium-plated plastic
Rust cannot upset plating on plastic surfaces, of course. However, because plastics are electrically non-conductive, the metal plating relies on electro-static attraction for its bond. This remains strong unless the thin plating is punctured. If that happens, it will very soon peel off entirely. There is no

69 Opposite: Chrome is a good metal to use in combination with ultra-modern and older furniture styles. Here, a stylish breakfast nook is composed of traditional wooden dining room chairs, a chrome and glass table and a half-globe, hanging chrome lampshade. The simple lines are complemented by the black and white colour scheme.

Right: Many quaint items are made of silver or silver plate – from ornate photograph frames and unusual tableware to clocks and hip flasks! Pewter things are usually large and simple, like coffee pots or mugs.

known cure for this, short of replating, and it is not worth replating cheap plastic objects.

Replating
Replating is not just a question of flashing an isolated patch with a new metal surface. It involves stripping the old plating completely, usually by shotblasting, repolishing the stripped surface and putting on all three plating layers afresh – to a standard appropriate to the intended use of the article. Much of the cost is accounted for by the work involved in obtaining a new, bare, highly polished, original metal base for the electro-plating process. You can, therefore, expect it to rise steeply with the object's size and weight.

Silver of sorts
Pure silver is very rarely met with, partly because it is expensive and partly because it is very soft and pliable. It is normally alloyed with baser metals such as copper and zinc, making a stronger, more hardwearing metal. The proportion of silver in these alloys is given in terms of parts of silver per 1,000 of the alloy. This proportion is known as 'fineness'. Sterling silver has a fineness of 925 – it contains 92·5 per cent silver and 7·5 per cent other metal.

Whatever the quality of the workmanship, solid silver articles now command high prices on the secondhand market, simply as sources of a scarce material. Things made of a silver alloy are slightly more common, but still relatively expensive. Indeed, few secondhand items are likely to consist of silver alloy throughout, but will be silver plated instead.

Silver plate
Most common and reasonably priced silver goods will have been electroplated after they were made. Signs of copper showing through worn patches indicate that a thing is plated, as do the stamped letters: EPNS (Electro-Plated Nickel Silver, an alloy of copper, zinc and nickel). Spoons and forks are almost invariably plated with this silver-coloured metal because it is hardwearing.

Removing tarnish
Left to itself, silver eventually turns black because of the film of silver sulphide which forms on it. Whether you use a slightly abrasive special cleaner or one of the dip-in solvents, you inevitably remove a thin layer of the silver every time you polish. Do it only when you have to, and then only sparingly. Chased lines should not be scraped clean: they are supposed to retain some tarnish. Very intricately chased pieces should be cleaned with one of the polishes which is easy to get out of the crevices and will not leave a thick deposit of white cream. If there are heavy, noticeable deposits already embedded in the crevices, a stiff scrub with an old toothbrush before cleaning will remove the worst.

Pewter pots
Other things are made from pewter, of course, but pots or dishes are the most common items made from this alloy of lead and tin (and occasionally other materials). These items are always solid pewter, which is cleaned just like brass, copper or zinc. If your chosen polish instructs you to buff the metal to a shine before the polish is quite dry, there may well be a waxy residue left on the surface. This should be washed off thoroughly before drinking or eating out of a pewter utensil. Otherwise, there is little to worry about, so long as you do not put a pewter item on a hotplate, provoking it to melt.

FIRST AID FOR CHINA

Judging from the contents of the average antique shop, old pottery, earthenware, and porcelain china must be the most plentiful relics of bygone ages in existence. The sheer fragility of the finer items, however, must mean that their ranks are steadily reducing in numbers and that you are unlikely to be able to replace a damaged piece with a similar one if it was made some time ago.

In any case, whether you originally bought it or whether you inherited it, your pretty or useful treasure (perhaps both) probably has a sentimental value for you out of all proportion to its monetary value. The vast majority of rare pieces will long since have been tracked down and had their whereabouts charted by both professional and amateur hunters. If you smash or chip anything in this category, its repair is probably best left to the experts, who use skilled and specialized methods, like re-firing.

In the case of less pretentious pottery, there is quite a bit you can do at home, by simple methods, towards helping it back to a useful if not too active life.

Adhesives

Glues and cements formulated to stick broken edges of ceramic ware together were once made from shellac. Perhaps more successful were the hard-setting cement type, but no adhesives now on the market are stronger than those based on epoxy resin. These were originally developed for airframe construction, and have as good a grip on glass and smooth metal as they have on more porous substances.

Most of these glues have one grave disadvantage: they take an inordinately long time to set at normal room temperatures, some as long as three days. It is possible, however, to reduce the setting time to hours if the join can be subjected to moderate heat, say in a cool oven. When this is not practicable, use a variety of quick setting epoxy adhesive, such as that made by Borden. These have become available only comparatively recently, so you may have to search a little to find one.

Surface chips

Chips which are really craters in the surface, rather than pieces broken bodily from an edge, are easily filled with one of the many modelling compounds used by sculptors and industrial designers. Stickier and trickier to use is an epoxy adhesive with powder colours mixed in. Obviously you will not have to bother with the pigmentation if you are going to paint any design features back in after gluing. This is only of value when the design of the piece is relatively simple.

Edge chips

Epoxy adhesive is equally suitable to use for repairing damaged edges. It will fill the space very firmly once set, but since there is nothing to support it until it has set you will have a delicate application problem — not an insuperable one, just awkward. One way of providing temporary backing is to press a flat wad of putty or plasticine on to the surrounding sound surface, to give the adhesive a depression to fill, instead of a yawning gap. Both putty and plasticine contain quite a bit of oil, so should not give any trouble when you want to remove them.

Clean breaks

Fresh fractures involving no splintering or crumbling away are the simplest of all to mend, and the most likely to remain hidden when repaired. Adhesives for china and for pottery are generally colourless or white, and have always been so. Anything that shows up on a mended article as a dark line is not glue, but dirt.

Dirty edges

Dark line trouble occurs as a rule when a piece breaks along a previously mended join, or is left for a lengthy period between being broken and being repaired.

Previously glued breakages will give the greatest difficulty, because their edges will not allow a fresh adhesive toe-hold until all the old glue is off — and it just may have been an epoxy. Luckily, this is not very probable. However, if you try immersing the piece in near-boiling water (do not simmer it), acetone, ammonia, or methylated spirit and it proves immune to each in turn (not all at once), suspect the worst and abandon the attempt. Remember to wash off one solvent before you try the next, so that each gets a fair chance.

Once you have removed the old glue, a strongish solution of household detergent in hot water, with a small amount of domestic bleach dissolved in it (about an egg-cupful to the gallon) should leave clean edges. Deeply ingrained soiling will only come out after a prolonged soak. On exceptionally stubborn items, it is better to leave them submerged in the solution for weeks, rather than increase the strength of the bleach. Strong bleaches may leave crystal deposits in the porous clay, which would be difficult to get out and which might upset the adhesive.

Rinse thoroughly and dry off the clean edges before re-gluing.

Mending methods

Apply the adhesive sparingly; too much will not make for a neat join because the excess in between the mating edges would tend to keep them apart. In addition, once this excess is squeezed out it makes it difficult to see whether or not the pieces are cramped together properly.

Sticky tape of some kind will probably be the only feasible means of holding the parts close together for the requisite length of time, even five or six minutes being a bit of an ordeal by hand pressure alone. Cellulose clear tape will work well for short stints, but when you have to cramp something together for three days its adhesive may dry and its grip loosen a little. Professional repairers normally use a brown-paper tape (common office type). If you use this, bear in mind that it shrinks as it dries out: a very helpful property, provided there is tape on both sides of the join.

Cracked but not broken

Professional pottery restorers and others of stout heart can sometimes mend cracks running from the body of a piece to one edge without deliberately completing the fracture. If you feel you have nothing to lose, try pulling the crack a little wider to see if the trick is possible. Provided that it will open sufficiently to allow a bit of card, or anything stiff and thin, to be inserted to hold it open, adhesive can be worked stingily into it with a fine brush. Then release the wedge and tape the join.

Should you pull a bit too hard when springing the crack open, you will either be lucky and simply complete the break or you will be unlucky and produce further fractures. Attempting crack-springing repairs is never a sure thing. Always try to protect your hands when doing such work.

Putting the pattern back

However well a crack is mended, gaps may remain in the pattern or picture that are just too blatant to be ignored. Artist's acrylic or oil colours are both quite satisfactory to use over the adhesive, although the matching-in will be mainly a matter of trial and error. In any event it is worth the attempt since errors can easily be rubbed out with a rag dipped in the appropriate solvent for the paint you are using.

A clear lacquer is needed to replace the lost glaze, or at least the appearance of it. In the absence of one made specifically for the purpose, an acid-catalyzed lacquer will make an adequate substitute. It is both water-clear and heat-resistant, although the latter virtue is unimportant if you only intend to display the piece.

Enamelware

True enamel consists of glass, in the form of coloured powder, which has been fused on to the surface beneath it by the application of heat. When enamel is chipped, it presents one of the most difficult repair problems. No paint can imitate its effect properly and refiring to add new enamel is out of the question because the old enamel could not withstand the necessary heat.

The only substance which can be applied cold and which will set to anything approaching an enamel surface is a liquid plastic sold mainly in kits for hobbyists, such as that made by Enamelcraft. It acquires its gloss as it flows to find its own level. To make it stable on an uneven surface, you must let it partially set first.

Being a plastic, the 'paint' can embody powder colour, but not necessarily with predictable results. It does, however, offer an interesting way of transforming dull earthenware that is not enamelled to begin with.

70 Right above: Do not be hasty and discard a favourite plate or pretty jug if it becomes cracked or chipped. With patience most repairs can be made without leaving noticeable scars. Right below: Broken handles on cups and mugs are one of the most frequent mishaps with china. They are easy to mend if the break is a clean one. Make sure no glue or grease remain round the break, and use an epoxy resin adhesive for the repair. To support a simple break while the adhesive sets use clear sticky tape, fixed crosswise and lengthwise around the handle. If it is broken in two places, try supporting it with plasticine as well. Broken plates can be supported underneath with an identically shaped plate greased so it can be easily removed when the adhesive dries.

MIRROR AND GLASS TO REFLECT UPON

Glass is a crystalline material. When it is clean and new this is not too apparent, but with advancing age and consequent exposure to the ravages of the environment it gradually becomes more brittle and more obviously crystalline.

This, however, is only one reason that glass loses its clarity. Another is that the surface (which is actually slightly porous) tarnishes and darkens when it comes under attack from chemicals in the atmosphere, smoke, light, running water and contact with other materials.

Kinds of glass

Molten glass may be formed into solid lumps by pouring into very simple moulds, cast into more intricate shapes in complex moulds, drawn into rods or tubes, rolled into thin sheets or blown into hollow forms, with or without the assistance of moulds. Additives can colour it, harden, soften or toughen it.

It is almost always possible to judge the delicacy of a glass item just from its appearance.

In the secondhand field, most of the inexpensive glassware you find will be fairly thick-walled blown glass, or heavy plate glass, in mirrors, for example.

Repairs to glass

Cracks, breaks, chips and scratches are more difficult to deal with in glass than in a material like china because glass is so hard all the way through. Besides this, to be successful the repair must not affect its translucence.

For this reason, surface chips are most difficult to fill invisibly. Luckily, the only fault in aged glass which is impossible to repair is a deep scratch. Almost every other trouble is capable of at least a partial solution.

Cracks

Cracks can be mended with an epoxy resin adhesive in much the same way as porcelain and the other ceramics, but it is always a wise precaution to clean the mating edges very thoroughly with methylated spirit before applying the adhesive. This is done to eliminate any trace of grease or oil, both arch-enemies of good adhesion, especially where epoxy and metal or glass are concerned.

Since most sticky tapes will not adhere well to a glass surface, give the same treatment to any surfaces which you must support with tapes. It should improve the adhesion.

Filling chips

If you want to attempt filling chips in glass, try a liquid plastic of the type sold for embedding things. It comes in a clear form but will take colours. Exact matching may present problems. The hobby varieties, such as Plasticraft, are very powerful adhesives, so will stay put without difficulty if you let the hardener begin its action before application.

Although it is possible to handle the hardened plastic after twenty-four hours, ideally it needs a week to

cure before it sets to its fullest extent.

Liquid plastic will come off your hands easily enough if you allow it to dry crisp and then rub hard. Removing it from anything else is like trying to get a limpet off a rock at low tide.

If you do not particularly want to tackle chip filling yourself, you can have them ground out professionally, at your own risk. The cost will probably be quite high because it is a skilled and time-consuming job.

Discoloration

When glass has tarnished or darkened, consider whether the patina really needs to be removed. You may want to retain an antique look about the article for some reason. If you do decide that the discoloration is nothing but an

71 Opposite: Transform a room's appearance with a nicely shaped mirror and an old frame, painted in an eye-catching design. Right: Glassware lends itself well to paper cut-out decoration. Known variously as découpage or decalcomania, it is an imaginative way to make lamps or vases from old bottles and jars.

ugly nuisance, you must take off the soiled top layer of glass, to reach the clean, untarnished glass underneath it. Chemicals such as ammonia may dissolve staining, but the eroded glass surface they produce will not be dissolved with it. There is no safe way for the average person to dissolve glass.

Fine abrasives are the best home solution for an eroded glass surface. Try metal polish, toothpaste, jeweller's rouge, or car-body rubbing compounds, but not scouring powders.

Mirrors
Most of the mirrors on old furniture will be tarnished in front and de-silvered behind, good for neither use nor ornament. Unless there is some decorative feature on the face, or the whole mirror has an elaborate and unreproducible form, it will most probably be both economical and practical to buy a new mirror, rather than go to the trouble and expense of having an old one resilvered.

If you do decide to have a mirror reconditioned and it is to be fixed in place with screws, have any necessary screw holes drilled through it at the same time. It is not difficult to drill holes through the glass yourself, but in the case of a mirror you run the risk of removing part of the silvering in the process.

Drilling holes in glass
For drilling holes in glass, a firm, dispensable base to lay the glass on, or a specially designed (by you) support for a bottle or other unstable form, a hand drill and a spear-pointed or triangular-tipped drill are the basic essentials. If you can arrange to have a water tap running gently on the drill as you work, so much the better. If you are drilling an old mirror, omit the water lubricant in case it should damage the silvering. The special drill has a tungsten carbide tip, only a little bit softer than a diamond, so there is no need to exert overmuch pressure or to turn the handle fast and furiously.

Work carefully and steadily. Rinse the glass dust away if you can. If you cannot, at least flush the hole out with a little water (or methylated spirit if it's an old mirror) Trand mop up the drillings with a wad of wet cotton wool.

Cleaning untarnished glass
Methylated spirit is quick and effective to use for cleaning glass, but

absolutely taboo where you have French polished wood around the panes — as you might on a display cabinet. Liquid metal polishes may also attack French polish, but try them first on small, inconspicuous areas. You may be lucky. Do not use any non-transparent cleaner on frosted or non-reflective glass or you may leave traces. Matt picture glass is quite fragile so always handle it carefully.

Jars and globes with découpage
Glass containers of most shapes and sizes can be decorated in a personal and fascinating way by using the art of découpage. To achieve this effect, the glass object must have a hole through which you can position cut-out pictures. Almost any kind of picture

or pattern is suitable, so long as its visible surface will take a clear adhesive.

Once you have spread the glue thinly over the picture surface, use bits of stick, bent wire or anything else which will enable you to position the pictures inside the container. The task can be frustrating, but the final result is well worth the painstaking effort.

To complete the process, pour emulsion paint into the jar or globes, swill it around until it covers all the unpictured glass, then pour it out. Inevitably a bit of paint will dribble between picture and glass here and there, but if you have fixed the pictures securely to the glass, this should not be enough to mar the final effect.

FRAME-UP

Left to themselves, picture frames will perform their function with little trouble. Old age catches up on them in the fullness of time, causing the wood to shrink and the glue to lose its grip, but it is rare for one to give way suddenly and unload its contents on to the floor.

Picture frame repairs

If you go hunting for secondhand frames to buy at bargain prices, however, you are bound to find an abundance of unloved and ill-treated ones. Naturally a hard life can loosen the corner joints of the stoutest frame. In general you should find that the bigger frames last better than the smaller ones, as they would have been made to support heavy loads of glass and canvas.

Where there is no splitting or breaking away of the wood, corner joints can often be held together with another nail or two and a little fresh glue, possibly without taking any of the other joints apart. The glue would have to be hot-melt, woodworking adhesive, such as Scotch glue – more modern ones having no affinity for that already in the wood.

It's also asking for trouble to use bigger nails than the originals. If you are convinced that there is not enough sound wood to hold small ones, it is far better to drill pilot holes and substitute a fairly long brass screw. If you adopt this method, sink the screw deeply enough below the wood surface to allow for filling later.

Tightening old joints

Slighter, smaller frames are usually held together by simple, mitred joints, the members being butted together, pinned and glued. Better-class frames, in the larger sizes at least, have proper fitted joints – open mortice and tenon, or halved – modified to incorporate the necessary mitres.

These joints tend to loosen when the wood has dried out through age or modern heating, or when the glue has decayed. One effective cure for this is to take the whole frame apart, clean up all the joint surfaces and cramp them together again, repacked with a PVA wood glue and scraps of thin veneer to compensate for the shrinkage.

It is possible to buy frame cramps quite cheaply, made from plastic and nylon or terylene cord. They are quite simple to make as well, consisting simply of four L-shaped pieces of wood held tightly in to the corners of the frame by a strong cord running all the

way around. Notches in the corner apexes stop the cord from slipping off. It can then be tightened with a short length of wood which acts as a tourniquet.

Provided that the inside angle of each corner-block is a true 90°, the frame will be pulled into a decent rectangle in this way. You can pin the joints instead, but it is more difficult to keep them square. Nevertheless, you may have to use very small nails or panel pins if the frame is ornate.

Cutting a frame to size

To reduce the size of a large frame simply measure the size of the picture to go in it, unfasten two diagonally opposite corners and cut all four sides down to the appropriate size. You will probably need to use a mitre box to get accurate angles. Re-glue the corners and clamp firmly until dry. Use a try-square to see that each corner is a right angle.

Patching up the decoration

Sometimes only a very small portion has been knocked out of the superimposed moulding and sculpture on a frame. If you think you can bridge the gap with a reasonably accurate imitation of the design, fill it in with a cellulose or resin filler and carve in the missing detail when it has set hard.

Long stretches are better if replaced entirely with modern plastic moulding, which may have to be substituted for the original decoration on all sides.

Frame finishes

It may very well be that you liked the look of your ornate frame before you patched it up, and do not want it to look brash and new. Be that as it may, the fillings and patches must be painted if they are not to stick out like sore thumbs. The best way of blending them in is to repaint the entire frame the same colour. Using a darker shade of gold paint, or dulling it down with a little bronze colour from the same range might help to soften the effect, but if that is insufficient you may have to fall back on deliberate aging techniques.

Gentle scrubbing of dirt into the crevices of the moulding with a soft brush is quite effective. Exposure to bright sunlight is also a good method, although it takes time and cannot be done with the picture in situ. Dullness without dirtiness may be enough to take off the rawness of new colour. Matt, rather dark tinted varnish painted on top of the gold could accomplish this much.

Plain wooden frames which have had new wood inserted respond well to dust rubbed on with a dark-coloured wax polish. Remember, the disguise does not need to be total, so long as you can remove the sharpness from the dividing line between the new and the old.

New wood can be given a soft patina in a very short time, by purposeful rubbing with a scrap piece of smooth hardwood, preferably harder than the wood it is treating.

Reglazing a frame

Fitting a new piece of non-reflective glass in a frame makes sound sense, even if the existing glass is still unbroken, because the fine surface etching eliminates all specular reflection and allows the picture to be seen clearly from virtually any angle.

Non-reflective glass needs two sorts of special care: handle it gently because it is rather thin; and remember where you put it down because it has no shine to make it obvious and you could easily lean your hand on it by mistake. Fragility makes it inadvisable to trim edges to fit, so measure accurately, allowing up to an extra millimetre all around for clearance.

The glass goes into the frame rebate first (underside of the frame), then the mask if there is one (perhaps for a print or photograph), then the picture itself. Unless the back of the picture already comes flush with that of the frame, packing must go in so that the final covering of brown paper over the back of the picture can lie smoothly, and be fixed to the edges with brown-paper tape. Thin polyether foam makes a safe packing.

Display frames

You may come across deep frames with stiff backboards on which pretty or interesting collections of objects can be mounted for display. If they can be pinned on, like butterflies, a special hardboard is available which is made to hold pins.

Plywood backboards can be covered with fabric, or painted. Fixings must suit the displayed item, of course. Some solid items can be screwed into the board and so anchored from the back. Others may have to be sewn or tied, or fastened with adhesive.

Alternative jobs for frames

Without a picture or other content, a frame may be considered simply as a surround, defining and enhancing a plain or patterned panel. Some of your ideas for exploiting the focusing power of a frame may involve putting strains on its structure that it was never intended to withstand. If, for example, you want to use a large frame to edge a bed-head panel or to act as a surround for a glass-topped coffee table, you should make sure that the backing boards make up in rigidity what the frame may lack.

With this proviso, almost anything is possible. If a frame is to carry loads without the support of a backboard, some strengthening should be given the corners. Steel or brass L-plates screwed to the back could be the simplest reinforcement to use.

1. to 3. If you want to strengthen the corners of a frame without dismantling it, you can drill diagonally through the corner pieces and glue in wooden dowels. You might also try screwing diagonal or triangular corner plates of plywood or metal at the back of a damaged frame.

4. To refasten the corners of frames, glue and then tie them with string as shown, until the glue sets. Use a PVA woodwork adhesive for best results.

5. & 6. Small pieces of broken moulding on frames can be repaired with plastic wood. Larger pieces can be replaced by taking an impression with modelling clay from a sound section of moulding. Use cellulose filler paste to make a cast of this. Sand down rough edges and glue the new piece in place with an epoxy resin glue.

7. Wax gilts make excellent substitutes for gold leaf when regilding a frame. Simply rub the wax on with a finger or cloth; a small stiff brush should be used to reach cracks and crevices. Protect this gilt with some type of clear alcohol-based varnish.

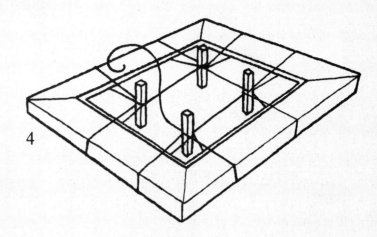

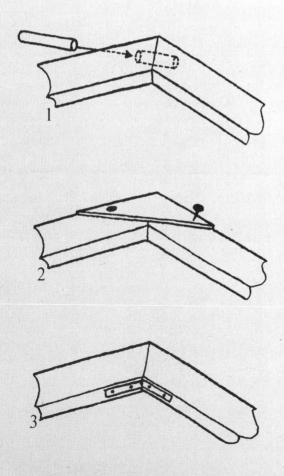

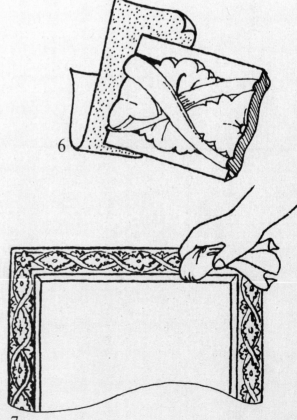

THE INSIDES OF THINGS

Has-been furniture made originally to contain things may never have been finished properly on the inside. The men who made it were not skimping or idle, but simply suiting whatever lining they used to its intended task.

Lining boxes, chests and small caskets was then and is now a trade in itself, quite separate from that of making containers. Only rarely will you be able to retain an original lining, which in any case may be badly deteriorated. Even sound linings may have been removed to allow the outside to be properly renovated. Usually, it cannot be put back, and the finish underneath it will almost certainly be unfit to take a new, sealed finish, without a great deal of preparation.

Modern materials, fortunately, offer tremendous advantages over older types – and they require little expertise in application.

Small boxes and cases
Cushioning and colour are usually the important attributes of lining materials used for small containers, rather than exceptional resistance to wear or damp. Baize, felt and padded silk were the traditional inner surfaces, and sometimes velvet or an imitation of it. Modern synthetic fabrics such as nylon, and imitations of leather in PVC vinyls, can provide hardwearing interiors if you especially need them. Padding is easily achieved with foam rubber or plastic.

Self-supporting materials such as felt and self-adhesive velours can be fixed directly on to the sides, lids and bottoms of small boxes, since you can cut them accurately to fit before having to glue them in place. For something like a cutlery case, you can make a far more professional job, and one more in keeping with its character, by using velvet material. However, you will have continual trouble with fraying edges if you simply stick it straight on to the box. The classic way is to mount each small panel separately, before putting it into place.

Cut thin, stiff, supporting pieces of cardboard for the panels, each one slightly smaller all around than its respective panel. To achieve the optimum precision, cut the pieces of card to size with a modelling knife or scalpel and steel ruler, rather than

scissors. The corresponding pieces of velvet must be cut with enough spare material to wrap neatly over the card without any overlap of velvet-on-velvet at the back. Corners are notched out of the velvet to avoid the same trouble. Glue is applied only between the back flaps of velvet and the back of the card, so there is no danger of staining the velvet where it will be seen once the panels are fixed in place. Use a flexible-bond adhesive, such as Copydex.

Adhesive should be applied over the whole back area of each panel, but sparingly, to avoid accidental oozings that might mar the finished appearance. The instructions which accompany the adhesive will probably advise coating both surfaces, allowing them to dry somewhat and then bringing them together. This procedure produces an impact adhesive, which you do not really need for this job. Instead, coat the fabric panel and press it gently into place while the adhesive is still tacky. If you do decide to use the impact adhesion method, you cannot afford to make the slightest error when positioning the panels – once the two glued surfaces touch they will bond.

If you would prefer a cushioned look – thin layers of plastic foam can be sandwiched between card and fabric. A buttoned effect is easily obtained by stitching through the fabric and foam. Obviously you will need to allow for the extra thickness of the padding when cutting the card. If you do not want a buttoned effect, stick the foam to the card, but not the fabric to the foam.

Large drawers and shelves
Linings for these shelves and drawers are rarely seen, so new ones can be chosen for their sheer practicality. PVC self-adhesive sheeting is a natural choice, but vinyl-faced wallpaper comes a close second – since it does not have to be stuck down.

To get an accurate fit with these sizeable pieces it helps first to cut a brown-paper template. Its edges can be folded and refolded to get an exact fit into angles and corners. Even self-adhesive materials, which can be cut to fit before the backing is taken off, benefit from the use of a template.

72 Above: Paper, felt, hessian and other fabrics make practical and good-looking linings for household containers. Opposite: Line both the inside and the outside of furniture to imitate the surrounding decor.

Wallpaper linings
The inside surfaces of large cupboards, wardrobes and bookcases are ideal sites for relatively small amounts of exotically patterned or super-costly wallpaper which you would not usually use on walls or ceilings. Shops frequently have odd remnant rolls for sale at special low prices after stocktaking – never enough for a room, but ample for a wardrobe. Few old-fashioned wardrobes will have sheer sides or backs, so templates also help here to fit the panels precisely.

It may be difficult or inadvisable to use standard wallpaper adhesive for this application, so try a simple test on a small corner of the wood to see if the varnish or other finish reacts. If it does, filled resin emulsion types, such as Clam 143, are often a good alternative choice.

Wallpaper, especially richly coloured or textured, shows to excellent advantage on the inside backs and sides of glass-fronted bookcases or other show-cupboard pieces. The idea is far from new, but not as widely used as it should be. Remember that it will be protected from the soiling that normal wallpapers are subjected to, so constant redecoration will not be necessary.

Wallpaper patchwork
Panels are small areas to deal with compared with walls and ceilings, so it is perfectly feasible to work original arrangements of paper patchwork on them to create a striking and unique decor.

It's rather difficult to work in situ on what can be quite a fussy job. Unless the arrangement is very simple, cut out a perfectly fitting backing sheet to allow the whole design to be pre-fabricated on a flat surface.

Patchwork may at first seem a rather haphazard method of decoration but the most effective and arresting designs are anything but that. Bold and simple themes are much more likely to be successful than busy, detailed patterns. Simple geometrical designs in contrasting shades of fairly plain paper are both easy to do and striking to look at. Hexagonal patches in random groups will also stand out well.

You will find it easier to make a patchwork if you cut the pattern from a solid template, made of thin sheet metal or plastic laminate. Set the template in place over the wallpaper and using its edges as a guide, cut out the shape with a fine knife. Naturally, you should not do this on the carpet. Hardboard makes a good cutting base. Let light colours predominate in the pattern. It will be easier to see things inside, especially if the unit is itself in a dark area.

Fabrics as linings

Fabric linings can be just as effective as wallpapers, but it should not be fixed permanently to the interior of a unit unless they are paper-backed — like proprietary hessian coverings. Cleaning or replacement will eventually be necessary for all linings, and it will be easier if the material is not permanently fixed.

All the same, fabrics normally have a softer texture than papers and can make interiors look especially inviting. The fabric can be mounted on sheets of thin hardboard which are cut to fit the units. Wrap the material round the panel and fix it at the back, as for the smaller cutlery box panels. The hardboard panels are simply held in place with small brass screws and screw caps, which enable them to be removed very quickly for cleaning.

USELESS TO USEFUL

In your searches for usable second-hand things you may well find many an item put aside long ago because the purpose for which it was created no longer exists. Either because they were solidly constructed or because they have had little use, many will still be in fine condition, ready to put in a lifetime of service for anyone with the imagination to find a use for them.

Old barrels

Beer now travels more often than not in modern metal containers, which are lighter, more hygienic and rarely need repair. Every now and again a supply of old oak barrels is disposed of in favour of the metal ones. If you are lucky enough to get hold of one of these it can be made into a serviceable and novel outdoor table.

No amount of rainwater is likely to affect oak badly, but it will retain its appearance better if you stand the barrel on a hard level base, made to drain effectively. Most barrels will collect water in the top of the lid, so either drill through the rim or notch it to allow the water to drain away. If you like the look of the wood as it is, leave it unfinished or give it a matt polyurethane varnish. If you feel it is too drab, paint it bright colours with a polyurethane finish.

Oak barrels are pretty heavy, and consequently quite stable, but if you find the top too small for the number of people who are to use it, add a false table top in exterior quality blockboard, such as the Cresta brand. This can be screwed to the barrel's lid, but remember to use bright zinc-plated screws to avoid rusting. Should the new top tend to make the barrel tip, stabilize it by filling wholly or partially with sand or stones.

Victorian mantels

Some of these elaborate structures of wood, marble, metal and glass are very gracefully proportioned and contain useful little features like shelves, drawers, hanging-hooks, mirrors, and occasionally even built-in frames for photographs. Usually well-built and quite strong they come on the market only too rarely. If you are looking for a mantel, try to salvage one from a house due for demolition.

If you are lucky enough to find such a piece, but do not have a fireplace of the right scale for it, consider turning it into a bedhead.

If its finish is in poor condition, or unsuitable for this new situation, you may have to apply a new one. If the wood or metalwork is at all ornate, try to avoid stripping the piece – it will be a difficult task.

A mantel will probably last longer if you screw it to the wall. Then the bed can still be moved for cleaning but the mantel will not get pulled around. Another advantage of fixing it permanently or semi-permanently to a wall is the possibility of fitting it with lights. Tasteful lamps, in character with the style of the headboard, would add greatly to its charm and usefulness.

Coal scuttles

Among the more plentiful items available from yesteryear are metal coal scuttles, some of them made of very good quality materials. The better looking ones were intended to stand in living rooms, and are consequently worth having for their appearance alone, whether or not you put them to work. In many cases, there may be opportunities to give them back their old job, although you might prefer to clean yours out thoroughly, polish and lacquer it, and use it as a magazine rack.

Wooden scuttles are rarer, so much so that younger people could pass them by, not recognizing them for what they are. Imagine a box, upright at the back and with a flat floor sloping up a little at the front edge, to stop the coal from falling out. The front edges of the side pieces sloped backwards quite steeply, parallel with the lid. A robust, often fussy handle sat on the lid. Another simpler handle was usually provided at the bottom edge of the lid. Most wooden scuttles were made from quite decent hardwood, and lined to some extent with steel or brass sheeting. Since they stood up to 450mm (18 inches) high, they were not the kind of things to lift up whenever you wanted to stoke the fire. A small shovel went with them for that chore.

Getting the inside of a wooden scuttle clean would not be half so feasible as scouring out a metal one. Uses to which you could reasonably put it would have to be very practical and unglamorous in character: make it into a shoe-cleaning unit, for example, and you might not even have to refinish it.

Tiffin table tops

The folding wooden underframe of a Tiffin table is more ingenious than robust, but nothing short of a furnace is likely to affect the thick, heavy-gauge brass top. These are about 600mm (about 24 inches) in diameter, and are flanged rather like a deep dinner-plate. Despite their Egyptian and oriental designs they were made primarily in England. When brightly polished they have a rich golden gleam that makes them highly effective

73 Opposite: A barrel with a stylized flower design adds a light touch to a shady corner of the garden.

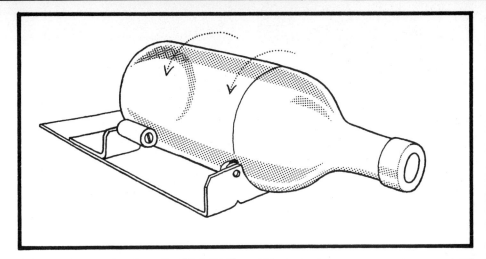

as wall plaques. Drill them through the centre and plug them to the wall with a single, 75mm (3 inch) brass screw.

Alternatively, you could mount it on a stand and use it simply to screen a little-used fireplace.

Washstand jugs

Porcelain, pretty and of generous proportions, these capacious jugs were quite common in country districts about 30 to 40 years ago. Modern plumbing has made most of them redundant, and their large capacity makes them unsuitable for everyday use as pitchers. But they are wide-necked, stable and strong, and so can be most useful as umbrella stands, or as brush-holders in the toilet, instead of the light and unsteady modern plastic ones.

Failed refrigerators

Scrap an old refrigerator and you may discard a very solid and serviceable cupboard, which possesses the virtue of airtightness. However, they should *never* be left empty, or used to hold children's playthings. Children are very tempted by old refrigerators, but because they are both airtight and impossible to open from the inside, they are very dangerous if children shut themselves in. If you are not going to make use of an old refrigerator, always break the lock or take the door off.

Perhaps the safest use for an old refrigerator would be as the long-term storage cupboard for soft fruit, such as apples or pears. When kept in a confined space, they slowly choke themselves in the carbon dioxide they give off. This gas, heavier than air, settles around them, keeping their skins from the oxygen in the air that would induce them to rot.

Most refrigerators have slatted shelves of plastic-covered wire ideal for holding rows of fruits, but supplementary racks might be needed to take full advantage of the available space. Beading supports to hold the extra shelves may be stuck to the sides with an impact adhesive.

Colander to lampshade

Old metal colanders adapt themselves well to life as lampshades. They are the right shape, they have the necessary perforations to let hot air escape, they can be attractively painted and they need very little in the way of adaptation.

If your lampholder is made of metal or is in poor condition it is advisable to replace it with a modern plastic one. Establish the diameter of the hole you need to make in the colander by

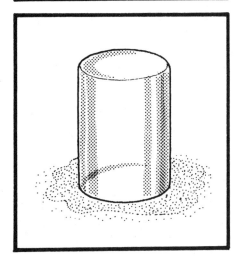

measuring the diameter of a hole in an existing lampshade.

To cut the hole in the colander, use a 'hole saw'. This consists simply of a twist drill bit with a plastic or metal collar around it which holds a specially formed piece of hacksaw blade. Once the central hole is made, the hacksaw bit acts rather like a pastry cutter. To prevent the cutter from bending the edge of the metal, support the colander on a block of wood.

Remember, when you come to decorate it use a heat-resistant paint.

New things from old bottles

Old bottles in an enormous variety of shapes and sizes are so easy to find.

Bottle cutters, available at handicraft shops or through mail-order firms, come in many forms. One type is described in the text, another (Ephrem's Olde Time Bottle Cutter) is shown above.
1. Remove the cap, then place the bottle on the cutter.
2. Lightly roll the bottle towards you, making one full turn.
3. Hold a lit candle under the line and turn the bottle in one direction slowly, then quickly.
4. Rub an ice cube over the heated line. To separate, pull lightly. Never force the pieces apart; repeat the heating process and try again.

Imagine what interesting articles could be made from bottles, if only they could be sliced across: vases, ashtrays, drinking vessels, rings, funnels, perhaps? The usual method of cutting sheet glass — scoring a line on one side, then flexing the sheet away from it on either side so that it gives way on the groove — proves to be useless on bottles.

New devices have recently been developed which solve the problem and crack bottles in predetermined places. These tools are known under various proprietary names, such as Bottle Chopper. It is a wise precaution to wear specially designed safety glasses while working.

74 Sewing machine tables are effective indoors or out.

Strictly speaking, such bottle cutters are two tools, not one. The first consists of a jig which is anchored in the bottle neck. This jig uses the neck as a centre to guide a special glass cutter around the outside of the bottle at any pre-set height. The next step is trickier, but enjoyable. This time, you use a small weight, swung from the bottle's neck so that it will hammer precisely behind the score line. The 'hammer' dangles inside the bottle, where you induce it to swing against the side, until a crack is produced. Continue tapping around the score line until a clean break occurs all the way around. Do not try to bend the glass off by hand.

Sharp edges are smoothed with oil-stones and a bit of fine oil. Finish off the edges with wet-and-dry silicon carbide paper, used wet.

Treadle sewing machine to table

In a sense, this conversion starts with a treasure — the graceful form of the cast iron under-frame. To make room for more than one pair of legs under the table, the treadle and connecting bar may have to go. Leave the wheel if you can, immobilized for safety.

Once you have removed the machine from the frame, you can lay on a new top, securing it with screws from underneath. If you would prefer to retain the original top, probably mahogany, a novel idea would be to fit a sheet of float glass accurately over it, with a photograph mounted under the section where the gap shows. There is a special printing paper for this purpose, which puts a positive transparency directly on to the glass.

OLD CLOCKS— NOT JUST A PRETTY FACE

There are so many different kinds of clock which you might encounter on the secondhand market that it is quite impossible to describe each in any detail. Here, we will deal in turn with three main types, the English fusee movement, the grandfather or long-case clock and finally, the carriage clock.

Principles of clock movements

The timing mechanism of a clock is known as *the movement*. The movement consists of a constant source of power — either a mainspring or weights — driving a number of gear wheels, which are known as *the train*. These in turn are controlled at their proper speed by the *escapement*. Escapements come in a number of designs but the most common are the anchor escapement, the lever escapement and the cylinder escapement. The complete clock is made up of the case, the movement, the pendulum and weights if fitted, the dial or clock face and the hands.

Clocks can be simple *timepieces* — by this it is meant that they do not strike or chime — or they can have a strike, or a strike and a chime. They may also be fitted with further refinements such as a repeat button — a knob which strikes the hour when pressed — and an alarm. A timepiece can be easily recognized by its single train and winding hole. A striking clock has two mainsprings, two trains and two winding holes. A chiming clock has three of each.

The gearing which transmits movement from the train to the hands is known as the *motion work*; the mechanism which permits the striking action is usually found under the dial and is known as the *strike mechanism*. Keeping these basic points in mind, let us proceed with more detailed descriptions.

The English fusee clock

Figure 1 illustrates an English fusee timepiece in a simple wood case. The back view of the clock is shown in figure 2. These clocks are very robust, have a cheerful loud tick and, when cleaned up with the case scraped and

75 On the table: Two striking clocks and a charming carriage clock; on the wall: two versions of the English fusee; and a splendid grandfather clock.

waxed, they make a charming addition to a wall. Fusee timepieces were made in their thousands and can still be found in shops, station waiting rooms and post offices. They are very reliable as clocks and can be regulated to a high degree of accuracy. The price of a shabby one can be extremely low, but one that has been polished up and is in working order will be five to six times as much.

Let us assume, therefore, that you have found an unloved specimen in a junk shop. What should you now look for? The first rule, which applies to all clocks, is 'do not be taken in by just a pretty case'. You should ensure that the movement can be repaired before you buy it, assuming, that is, that you want your find as a clock, and not just as an attractive ornament.

Examining the fusee clock

The clock must be examined properly. First, open the little trap-door in the side of the back, look in and see if the clock has a pendulum. If it has, unhook it (see figure 5) and take it out. If there is no pendulum, the clock may still be worth having, but it will cost at least half as much again as the clock itself to have a new one supplied and fitted.

With the pendulum out, place the clock on its back and open the glass which is usually hinged on the right side. Check the dial and hands for damage. Turn the hands forward to ensure that they are not broken or pinned loosely. Do not worry if they are not synchronized as this is easily put right.

There are specialists who can make any known part for a clock, who can make a new hand to match the one remaining and who can restore dials to their former glory. However, these things take time and money and you cannot undertake major repairs such as these by yourself. The best advice is to accept a clock with a broken glass – firms are available which will cut and bevel a new one for you – but steer clear of badly damaged hands and dials.

Checking the timing mechanism

Now to the movement itself. Having closed and secured the glass, place the clock face down on a bench. The box over the back is held in place by four dowel pegs. Remove these and lift the box off. You will now see the fusee (figure 3) from which the movement gets its name.

The fusee may at first seem complicated, but it is really a very simple mechanism. It was designed to ensure that the powerful mainspring gives a constant torque, or twist, to the train and does not fall off in power as the spring runs down. The power of the mainspring in the brass barrel is passed on to the fusee by means of a small chain or a wire line.

Once you have established that the fusee is in place, give the clock a short wind to impart a little power to the mechanism. Three or four clicks will do. If the fusee is of the chain type – it looks like a miniature bicycle chain – make sure that the chain is not broken. Chains can be repaired quite easily, but spare chains for replacement are very hard to find.

If the clock has a wire or gut line fusee, its condition is not so important, as spares are quite easy to purchase from special dealers in clock materials.

Now check the train wheels (see figure 4) for end and side shake. This should not be excessive. The train drives the *escape wheel* (figure 5) which is controlled by the *anchor*. With the pendulum off and the clock partially wound, the clock should tick fast when held in an upright position. Try this and, at the same time, observe that the hands are moving around the dial. If the train runs free, and the hands whirr around, there is something wrong with the escapement and it is advisable to look for another clock!

If the clock will not tick at all, this may be because the movement is very dirty. Move the crutch (see figure 5) from side to side and see if the escape wheel goes around. A busy tick is the best sign but, if the escape wheel turns a full 360° when you move the crutch by hand, the clock should not be too difficult to repair, although it will probably require expert attention.

The last thing to check is the pendulum. It should be straight, with a rating nut at the bottom and a suspension spring at the top. Suspension springs are often broken because the pendulum has not been unhooked in transit. However, their repair is simple and inexpensive. Similarly, a missing key for winding is no real drawback, as a dealer can easily supply one. Once your examination is complete, replace the back cover and begin to bargain with the shopkeeper.

The grandfather clock

The grandfather or long case clock is a beautiful piece of furniture, but make sure that you buy one which will fit into your house. It may seem silly to say this, but these clocks can be more than seven feet high.

Having learned how to examine a fusee timepiece, you should have no difficulty with a grandfather clock. The basic difference is that a grandfather is driven by weights, has a much longer pendulum and usually has a striking mechanism.

Face to face with the clock of your dreams, how do you look it over? Again remember not to be taken in by the case alone. Getting at the movement may seem to be something of a problem, however. The glass panels in the side of the case reveal

nothing. Do not be discouraged, it is really very simple.

Figure 6 shows how the entire hood of a grandfather clock slides forward. Open the door in the clock case and then the door covering the dial. If a catch is fitted, and often it is not, it should be on the left side of the dial door where marked. Sometimes the catch is a wooden lever operated from inside the door in the clock case. In any case try feeling for the hook with your fingers and then gently slide the hood forward until it is completely free. Be especially careful when doing this. Many an 'expert' has either dropped the hood or pulled the whole clock forward on top of himself!

The movement of a grandfather clock

Now to examine the movement. As before, start with the hands and dial, the only difference being that the movement remains in situ on the clock case. Turn the hands slowly in a clockwise direction. You should hear the strike mechanism released at the hour and possibly the half hour. Grandfather clock hands are often of an intricate design and it may be quite costly to have a broken one replaced.

If the weights of the clock are hooked on, you can test the train and escapement as for the fusee clock. If they are not, pull down on the gut lines – usually the right one as you face the clock is for the hands and the left one is for the strike. Simulate the weight in position by pulling. With a grandfather clock, you can leave the pendulum in place, swing it from side to side and watch the escape wheel revolve. If anything jams or locks, do *not* force it.

The strike mechanism is tested in the same way, but it can often be jammed. Pull on the left gut line, move the minute hand past the hour and watch the strike train revolve.

There are often parts of a grandfather clock missing. As a rough guide, pendulums, weights and bells for the strike can be obtained fairly easily at reasonable cost. However, missing gear wheels have to be redesigned and then made up and this can prove to be very expensive.

Setting up a grandfather clock

Finally, two points about setting up your clock when you get it home. Figure 7 shows three drawings which demonstrate how to secure the clock to the wall. This is very necessary, for unless the clock is held rigid, the vibration of the pendulum and the swing of the weights at the full length of their lines can cause the whole clock to sway in sympathy and bring the pendulum to a halt.

The second problem will be putting the clock in beat. Open the door of the clock case and allow the pendulum to hang still (see Figure 8). Mark

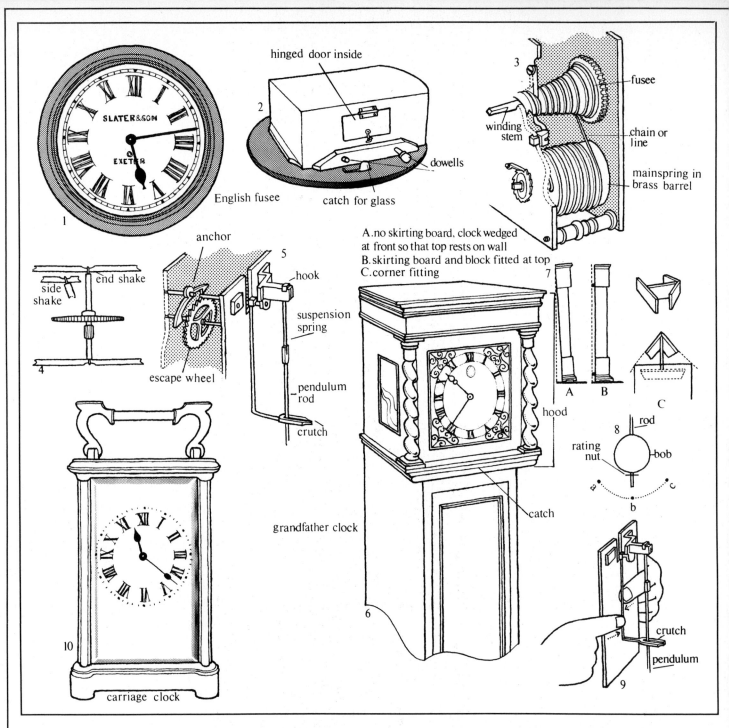

hinged door inside

English fusee

2

catch for glass

dowells

3

fusee

winding
stem

chain or
line

mainspring in
brass barrel

anchor

side
shake

end shake

escape wheel

4

5

hook

suspension
spring

pendulum
rod

crutch

A. no skirting board, clock wedged
at front so that top rests on wall
B. skirting board and block fitted at top
C. corner fitting

7

A   B

C

hood

8   rod

rating
nut

bob

a   c
b

catch

grandfather clock

6

crutch

pendulum

9

10

carriage clock

where the end of the pendulum (b) hangs. Dressmakers' pins stuck in the wood at the back of the case make a good mark. Swing the pendulum to one side till it ticks and mark this position (a). Swing to the other side (c) and mark again. The arcs ab and bc must be equal if the clock is to run properly. If they are not equal, bend the crutch (figure 9) until they are. For example, if it is necessary to move the pendulum more to the left, face the clock front and gently bend the crutch to the left. Adjust in slow stages, check the swing each time, and correct until the arcs are equal.

Finally, a point about regulating the speed of the clock. For all pendulums, the higher the bob, the faster the clock will go. To make it go faster, merely wind up the rating nut to lift the bob.

Carriage clocks

In the last few years carriage clocks have become very popular, so they may be difficult to find at bargain prices. A simple timepiece is illustrated in figure 10. More complicated clocks, striking on bell or gong with repeats and alarms, can be found but are rapidly becoming very expensive.

If you do find one, wind it up, hold it by the top handle and rotate it in a horizontal plane. You should see the balance wheel through the top glass panel swing from side to side. If the movement seems sound – you cannot get your fingers at it but you can look and see whether the wheels and hands rotate – do not worry too much about the state of the case or the glass panels. The case can be electro-gilded, as was the original finish, and panels can be cut, bevelled and

replaced. You must be prepared to spend a fair amount of money on these repairs, but once done they may double the value of the clock.

Cleaning a clock

Complete instructions for cleaning a clock are quite elaborate, but these are the basics. Take the movement out of the case. Remove the hands, the dial, and the motion and striking works. Let down the mainspring by releasing the click mechanism as you control the spring carefully with the key. Dismantle the rest of the clock. Clean all the parts in benzine and polish them with metal polish before reassembling. Clean the pivot holes carefully with an orange stick. Lightly oil the mechanism, wind the clock and then, if not successful, refer to a good manual on clocks.

BONE, IVORY AND TORTOISE-SHELL

Bone is at least one substance that suffers no shortage of raw materials for replacement of broken or missing pieces. A good-sized section of leg-bone from the butcher will yield a great deal of useful, solid cutting material. However, before you put it into store for future use in repair work, you must separate the hard bone from the meat, marrow and gristle scraps that come with it.

Mending bone
Stewing it for an hour or two will soften and loosen things enough to make it possible to scrape the outside clean and remove the marrow. After this initial scraping you may need to boil it a bit more in clean water to remove all the final traces.

Almost certainly, the clean bone will be too dark in shade for some of the applications that it will be needed for, but do not bleach it too white to begin with. Soak it in a cold, dilute solution of domestic bleach until it looks reasonably uniform in shade. Remove all traces of the bleach by rinsing the bone several times in very hot water. Store it in a very dry place.

Bone can be cut with a hacksaw, whittled with a drawing knife, filed, sanded and polished. Remember it has a 'grain' so you should cut repair inserts to match in properly. Quick-setting epoxy adhesives are the most practical to use for bone repairs.

Yellow ivory
The dividing line between what some regard as deep cream and others as yellow can be a hazy one. This, of course, makes it difficult to tell if ivory has discoloured from simple aging or from staining. The safest criterion is probably the distribution of the discoloration. Aging-yellow will be pretty even all over, while stains will be patchy and localized.

If the item is stained to a totally unacceptable degree, bleach it very gingerly with a dilute domestic bleach. Ivory is a natural material with grain and a tendency to fine cracking, which wetting might well precipitate.

Real tortoiseshell
Like ivory, tortoiseshell was originally grown by a living creature for its own protection. Do not let sunlight play on tortoiseshell if it is in good condition because even mild heat can dry it out

and the light can bleach it. If it is a little deteriorated, try wiping it over with any natural clear oil.

Should you fail to revive the surface by this means, rub the top layer with fine-grit paper (wet-and-dry or Lubrisil) until you get to sound tissue. Polishing gently with wax to finish is all you dare do on a fragile structure. Heavier ones can be buffed with a power drill, fitted with one of the small fabric dollies. Use the polishing compound supplied in the kit which comes with the dolly.

If you can, mount the drill and polishing wheel on a bench cradle and hold the article against it with both hands. Let the motor do the work and

76 Above: Horn beakers; an ivory-backed dressing table set; tortoiseshell napkin rings; a bone-handled carving set.

do not press hard. Keep the wheel moving over the surface of the tortoiseshell, to avoid over-heating it.

Knife handle repairs
Traditionally, these were fixed on by melting a bituminous filler into the handle socket and setting the pointed end of the blade into it. The fixing was very strong, but even so hot water loosens many good joints. To mend, drill out the old filler if you can, and replace it with car-body resin filler.

NEW LAMPS FOR OLD

Many unusual containers or cast-off items, such as old coffee-grinders or large, globular glass bottles, can be made into attractive lamps. Several basic techniques can be learned which will then apply to almost any lamp you will make.

Bulb holders

Most lamps can be made with one of two basic types of bulb holder. One is for fitting into bottle-necks and has a long, tapering 'cork'; the other is for screw-fixing to solid bases and has a hollow plinth with some thin segments moulded into the sides. These can be nicked out cleanly if you want to bring the flex out sideways.

If your chosen base is a bottle or some other hollow and not-too-heavy vessel, it is safest to use a bulb holder which has the flex coming out through the cork. Then you can drill a hole through the glass and lead the flex through it. Avoid using the type of bulb holder with flex coming through the side, above the bottle's neck. The weight of the cable can easily pull over all but the heaviest base and it is also impossible to conceal properly.

Of course, it is possible to increase a bottle's weight and to some extent its stability, by filling it with sand or marbles. However, if the basic shape of the bottle does not give it a low centre of gravity to begin with it will not be possible to balance it properly.

Screw-on bulb holders are especially useful for fitting bulbs to solid, flat-topped lamp stands. They can be mounted over a small hole so that the wire does not need to show; many have built-in switching mechanisms — a good feature to have in any lamp.

Drilling through block bases

The sheer mass and weight of solid-block bases made from lumps of stone, slate or similarly dense material, is sufficient to counteract an accidental pull on a cable. Nevertheless they would have to be extremely heavy to be regarded as totally safe in this respect.

Drilling a hole right through the block may seem a daunting prospect, and cannot be done at all without a power drill. It will need a tungsten-carbide tipped drill bit of a large enough diameter to make a hole the cable can comfortably fit through. The bit should also be long enough to bore through the whole block from top to bottom in a single pass: do not try to reverse and drill half the hole from the opposite direction.

Soft materials such as slate can sometimes be more difficult to drill through than harder ones, most of which can be penetrated by using an impact attachment. This is a simple device which makes the drill-bit deliver short, sharp, hammer blows as it rotates. Pulverizing action like this helps to get through concrete or other intractable materials, which would otherwise blunt or overheat the tip before any inroad has been made. Not all masonry bits will stand up to impact drilling, but getting one that will is mainly a matter of asking the dealer before you buy. Impact-proof bits will usually work equally well on purely rotary applications.

Adequate support for the block while you are drilling is very important for both effectiveness and safety. This is especially true if you try to drill diagonally to bring the flex out from the side of the block, as near to the bottom as possible. If you have qualms about your ability to achieve this, drill vertically down and straight through instead. To take the cable out, you will then have to file or chisel a shallow channel under the base.

Impact drilling should present no clogging or binding problems, but you may encounter them when going through soft materials. In general, these do not respond to the impact method and should be bored with a normal, rotary bit. Chips and dust tend to become tightly packed in the flutes of the drill, thereby clogging it up.

If you can see dust or chips appearing steadily from the hole, and the tone of the motor does not vary to any marked degree, there should be no problem. Listen for a drop in the motor-speed, and for screaming noises from the drill tip. Watch for the slightest bit of smoke, or smell of it, from the hole. The trick for the prevention of this clogging is to withdraw the rotating drill at regular intervals to clear the flutes and the hole. The stickier the material you are drilling, the more often you should do it. With practice you will learn to feel and hear when it is advisable to withdraw.

A chimney-pot lamp

Your ambitions need not be confined solely to lamps of table size. Although an object such as a chimney pot may at first seem a highly unlikely suggestion, there are one or two considerations that make it perfectly practical. Both its shape and weight would make it very steady. Being hollow, it would not present a drilling problem, only the much easier one of providing anchorage at one end for the bulb holder. Highly glazed or matt surfaces can be found with a little searching and if you do not like the natural colour, painting can work wonders in transforming it.

Of course, there is not the slightest need to block in the pot at its base as it will stand quite happily on its rim, but a flat filling or cap for the top

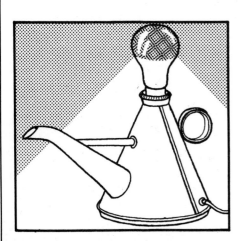

An oilcan lamp looks best with a crown-silvered bulb and does usually not require a lampshade.

Carboys, or any large globular bottles, make lovely lamps. Fit them with cork-style bulb holders.

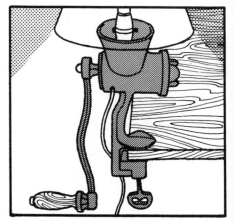

Meat mincers often make practical lamps for kitchens, as they are easy to fix on shelves.

is essential. This can be made on a once-and-for-all basis since it will never have to be removed. One way of capping the hole is to cut out two discs from hard wood, sticking them together to make a rebated 'cork'. The bottom one will have to fit inside the top as closely as possible so that resin filler or exterior grade cellulose filler can be packed around to hold it. Shape the top disc flush with the rim using a cabinet file or a medium grade abrasive paper.

An easier and probably neater method is to turn the pot upside-down on to a flat board and fill in the end to a depth of 50mm (2 inches) or so with a car-body resin filler or a proprietary cement filler. Place newspaper or plastic sheeting between the pot and the board to stop the filler from sticking. Both are quite easy to scrape off after drying, but a bit of grease on the upper surface of the plastic sheeting will avoid even that necessity. In any case, the filler will have to be sanded or filed smooth and flush with the top rim so that the bulb holder can be screwed in place. Before doing this, however, drill the chimney-pot to take the cable and paint it. Finally drill a hole in the wall of the pot near the base to lead the flex out and then fit the bulb holder and lampshade.

Solid wood bases
Whether these bases take the form of a smoothed and finished oblong or cube, or of a fat log, the difficulty lies in boring a hole down the grain. Always a troublesome operation, such drilling is rarely successful because there is never enough resistance to screw-action to give the auger a positive grip. The longer the hole and the less seasoned the wood, the more difficult it becomes.

Diagonal drilling is the shortest solution, probably starting from a point nearer the edge of the wood block to reduce the length of hole needed. Even this expedient, however, will need quite a long drill bit, one not readily available to the home craftsman.

There are two feasible do-it-yourself methods to choose from. If drilling by hand, you can get Scotch-eyed augers, which have a special hole going across the shank to take a special 'tommy'-bar. Enormous leverage can be applied with moderate effort. Otherwise hire a heavy-duty power drill that has a slow speed and a very powerful twist; drill very intermittently, preferably in a horizontal direction with the log anchored firmly to a bench. Clear chips often and carefully.

Oilcan lamps
Old-style oilcans sometimes have novel contours which will make intriguing shapes for lamps. Most that you find will be made from tinplate, rather heavy-gauge, and the seams will be prominent, folded over and brazed. Any oil remaining inside must be washed away. Methylated spirit is probably the safest solvent to use, although caution is still needed as it is flammable.

An oilcan lamp would probably look ludicrous if fitted with a shade, but you will still need to fit a fairly large bulb holder just to accommodate one of the smaller, screw-fitting, candle-style bulbs. Try to get one with a screw-collar, for which you can drill a hole approximately the right size and fix with epoxy or resin filler. When you lead out the cable somewhere near the bottom of the can, fit a rubber 'grummet' into the hole to stop the flex being cut: electrical suppliers stock them in assorted sizes. If the outer surface is still unattractive after you have cleaned it up, use an antique metallic paint to re-finish it.

Jar-type bases
Glass measuring jars normally have quite heavy bases which make them suitable for conversion into lamps.

77 Above: Plain lampshades can be decorated in numerous ways to dress up an old lamp. This one has been marbled using the techniques discussed earlier.

Their tops may be too wide for cork-type holders, so it may be necessary to make wooden lids for the screw-type holders.

Large carboy-style jars are often used to contain drinks such as draught cider. Their globular shape is very attractive and these bottles are little trouble to convert.

Plastic embedding kits can also provide good lamp bases. Use large, fat moulds which are available as additions to the basic kit.

Lampshade proportion
Generally, two basic requirements must be satisfied when fitting lampshades. First choose a shade which shields the eyes of the person sitting in the lowest seat in the room. Secondly, be sure that the shade is tall enough to keep the light from dazzling a six-footer when standing up. If you satisfy these conditions, the shade proportions should be accurate. If in doubt, choose a slightly oversize shade.

For a quaint-looking lamp, use an old coffee grinder, painted or varnished for a pretty finish.

Some of the most interesting shapes for lamps can be found in odd pieces of driftwood.

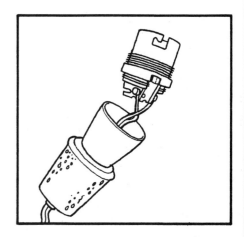

An exploded view of a cork-style bulb holder with the wiring attached.

MIX AND MATCH FURNITURE ARRANGE-MENTS

Rooms with a blend of furniture styles and finishes tend to be more interesting and warmer in feeling than those which do not mix-and-match. By acquiring an eye for colours and a strong sense of proportion it is possible to mix almost anything with a reasonable amount of success.

Opposites attract

It is a general rule that every furniture shape needs a counterpoint in order to be fully appreciated. In furnishings opposites *do* sometimes attract, and very effectively too. Low lines need the occasional tall shape; severe planes can be set off by some round, squashy shapes, such as large floor-cushions.

Split-level interior

A close look at this modern, split-level room will reveal that it has been furnished with a well-chosen mixture of modern and not-so modern pieces.

On the lower level the modern, light-wood rectangular tables have been paired with several traditional bent-wood chairs. These have been rubbed down smooth with a medium-grade abrasive paper and painted cheerful colours in gloss paints. A clear polyurethane lacquer finish over the paint will give the chairs excellent protection against scuffs and scrapes.

The armchair in the foreground has been re-upholstered in a smart-looking modern stripe which both flatters its curved high back and blends it in with the clean lines of the room.

The upper-level bedroom has been given a charming touch by the addition of the miniature pet's house in the left-hand corner and the iron-based oval table with the globular glass fish bowl on top. The pet's house could be finished in any number of ways, but here it has been left in its natural wood finish and given a good polish for protection. The iron-base of the table has had all traces of rust removed (see pages 102–103) and been painted a soft cream colour.

On the right the stool has been rubbed down with abrasive paper and then painted in a gloss-finish lime green to compliment the other greens in the room. A small round cushion was made to cover a scruffy-looking seat.

The kitchen

Pine and country-look furniture of almost any period is a popular choice for older style buildings with high ceilings and large rooms. In this kitchen, the furniture has been carefully stripped down and the natural wood surface left to view. If the wood is at all dry, it is advisable to rub in a coat or two of boiled linseed oil and finish with a good wax polish.

To complete the old-fashioned look in the room, the cabinet doors at the left were cleverly finished with old ceramic tiles. These were fixed in place with a synthetic latex adhesive.

Dining room

The very comfortable, plush look of this dining room has been created in part by the use of soft fabrics — even on the walls — and by the combination of beautifully finished natural wood tables and cabinets with the more casual cane and basketweave chairs and catch-alls.

The cane chairs were in good shape and needed mainly a good clean with a rag, brush and warm soapy water. Afterwards they were painted black using a spray gun; an aerosol would work just as well.

Besides the textures, the proportions of the various pieces work very well together — tall at the back wall, oval in the centre, and long rectangular along the right-hand wall.